Honouring and Admiring the Immoral

"A much-needed investigation into one of the hottest topics in philosophy, psychology, and public discourse"
– *Maria Silvia Vaccarezza, University of Genoa, Italy*

Is it appropriate to honour and admire people who have created great works of art, made important intellectual contributions, performed great sporting feats, or shaped the history of a nation if those people have also acted immorally? This book provides a philosophical investigation of this important and timely question.

The authors draw on the latest research from ethics, value theory, philosophy of emotion, social philosophy, and social psychology to develop and substantiate arguments that have been made in the public debates about this issue. They offer a detailed analysis of the nature and ethics of honour and admiration, and present reasons both in favour and against honouring and admiring the immoral. They also take on the important matter of whether we can separate the achievements of public figures from their immoral behaviour. Ultimately, the authors reject a "one-size-fits-all" approach and argue that we must weigh up the reasons for and against honouring and admiring in each particular case.

Honouring and Admiring the Immoral is written in an accessible style that shows how philosophy can engage with public debates about important ethical issues. It will be of interest to scholars and students working in moral philosophy, philosophy of emotion, and social philosophy.

Alfred Archer is an assistant professor of philosophy at Tilburg University and a member of the Tilburg Center for Logic, Ethics, and Philosophy of Science. His primary research interests are in moral philosophy and moral psychology, particularly supererogation, the nature and ethics of admiration, and the ethics of fame.

Benjamin Matheson is a Humboldt research fellow at Ludwig Maximilian University of Munich. He has research interests in ethics, moral psychology, philosophy of emotions, metaphysics, and the philosophy of religion. His work has appeared in *Philosophical Studies, American Philosophical Quarterly, and Canadian Journal of Philosophy*.

Routledge Focus on Philosophy

Routledge Focus on Philosophy is an exciting and innovative new series, capturing and disseminating some of the best and most exciting new research in philosophy in short-book form. Peer reviewed and at a maximum of 50,000 words shorter than the typical research monograph, *Routledge Focus on Philosophy* titles are available in both ebook and print-on-demand formats. Tackling big topics in a digestible format, the series opens up important philosophical research for a wider audience and as such is invaluable reading for the scholar, researcher, and student seeking to keep their finger on the pulse of the discipline. The series also reflects the growing interdisciplinarity within philosophy and will be of interest to those in related disciplines across the humanities and social sciences.

A Defence of Nihilism
James Tartaglia and Tracy Llanera

The Right to Know
Epistemic Rights and Why We Need Them
Lani Watson

Honouring and Admiring the Immoral
An Ethical Guide
Alfred Archer and Benjamin Matheson

**Newton's Third Rule and the Experimental Argument
for Universal Gravity**
Mary Domski

For more information about this series, please visit: www.routledge.com/Routledge-Focus-on-Philosophy/book-series/RFP

Honouring and Admiring the Immoral
An Ethical Guide

Alfred Archer and
Benjamin Matheson

Routledge
Taylor & Francis Group
NEW YORK AND LONDON

First published 2022
by Routledge
605 Third Avenue, New York, NY 10158

and by Routledge
2 Park Square, Milton Park, Abingdon, Oxon, OX14 4RN

Routledge is an imprint of the Taylor & Francis Group, an informa business

© 2022 Taylor & Francis

Library of Congress Cataloging-in-Publication Data
Names: Archer, Alfred, author. | Matheson, Benjamin,
author.
Title: Honouring and admiring the immoral : an ethical
guide / Alfred Archer and Benjamin Matheson.
Description: New York, NY : Routledge, 2022. |
Series: Routledge focus on philosophy | Includes
bibliographical references and index.
Subjects: LCSH: Honor. | Celebrities—Conduct of life. |
Character—Public opinion.
Classification: LCC BJ1533.H8 A68 2022 (print) |
LCC BJ1533.H8 (ebook) | DDC 179/.9—dc23
LC record available at https://lccn.loc.gov/2021018304
LC ebook record available at https://lccn.loc.
gov/2021018305

ISBN: 978-0-367-40714-8 (hbk)
ISBN: 978-1-032-06683-7 (pbk)
ISBN: 978-0-367-81015-3 (ebk)

DOI: 10.4324/9780367810153

Typeset in Times New Roman
by codeMantra

Contents

Acknowledgements

The idea for the book started in the spring of 2017 during Benjamin's TiLPS visiting fellowship. We noticed that philosophical discussions of immoral artists tended to focus on their works rather than our responses to immoral artists. The revelations of the autumn of 2017 and the subsequent #metoo movement made us realize our work might be even more important than we initially realized. We applied for further funding so that Benjamin could be a guest researcher on Alfred's NWO (The Netherlands Organisation for Scientific Research) project on "The Value of Admiration" (Grant Numbers 016.Veni.174.104 and 040.11.614). We are grateful to the Department of Philosophy at Tilburg University for having such a wonderful research environment in which we could explore and develop the ideas that are central to the book. Thanks also to the members of Tilburg's Emotions and Moral Psychology Reading Group for their contributions and critical inputs.

We are grateful to the NWO and TiLPS for funding that made our collaboration possible. Alfred is grateful for the NWO's initial funding of his Veni project which funded his work on this project. Benjamin is also grateful to Stockholm University and the Alexander von Humboldt Foundation for employment and funding that made his work on this project possible.

We have presented the central ideas of the book in Tartu, Madrid, Genoa, Delft, Utrecht, Tilburg, Stockholm, Maribor, Prague, Munich, and Leiden. We are grateful to audiences for their comments and feedback. In particular, we are grateful to the conversations we have had with the following philosophers, at these events or elsewhere, on topics related to this work: Marcel van Ackeren, Kenneth Aggerholm, Marina Barabas, Gunnar Björnsson, Daphne Brandenburg, Seamus Bradley, Christine Bratu, Huub Brouwer, Luke Brunning, Joanna Burch-Brown, Amanda Cawston, Sam Clarke, Matteo Colombo, Christopher Cordner,

Christopher Cowley, Willem van der Deijl, Yvette Drissen, Wim Dubbink, Lee Elkin, Bart Engelen, Helen Frowe, André Grahle, Robert Hartman, Caroline Harnacke, David Janssens, Sofia Jeppsson, Andrew Khoury, Ian Kidd, Tim Klaassen, David Levy, Pilar Lopez-Cantero, Elinor Mason, Christian Miller, Georgina Mills, Erich Hatala Matthes, Neil McDonnell, Heidy Meriste, Per Milam, Kian Mintz-Woo, Dorota Mokrosinska, Kamila Pacovská, Glen Pettigrove, Carolyn Price, Chiara Raucea, Mike Ridge, Natascha Rietdijk, Catherine Robb, David Shoemaker, Maureen Sie, Leonie Smith, Lotte Spreeuwenberg, Jan Sprenger, Alan Thomas, Lani Watson, Naftali Weinberger, Tom Wells, Nathan Wildman, Vanessa Wills, and Alan T. Wilson. Mark Alfano deserves special thanks here for attending at least five of our talks on this topic.

We have also discussed this work in classes at Ludwig Maximilians University of Munich, Tilburg University, Tulane University, and the OZSW Moral Psychology Winter School. Thanks to the students in these classes for their helpful feedback including: Alrun Bernhard, Brenda Breukers, Alexander Edlich, Cassandra Grützner, Jenny Janssens, Bram Medelli, Karim Nkrumah, Christianne Smit, Lotte Spreeuwenberg, Dominic Tschermy, Charlotte van Veen, and Scott Wolcott (apologies to the many students not mentioned here). Thanks also to Mark Alfano, David Shoemaker, Maureen Sie, and Tom Wells for facilitating some of these discussions. Alfred also had the pleasure of supervising student theses on related work by Mette de Brouwer and Jenny Janssens and would like to thank them both for their insights.

We have also both benefitted from discussing these and related ideas with academics from outside of philosophy including: Alice Bosma, Mark Brandt, Simon Frith, Carlo Garofalo, Marlies de Groot, David Matheson, Eva Mulder, Thia Sagherian-Dickey, and Ines Schindler. In particular, a very helpful conversation with Anna Paley and Rob Smith alerted us to some highly relevant literature at a crucial stage in the writing process.

Alfred would also like to thank Joanne Chung, Bart Engelen, Theo Klimstra, Anne Reitz, Jelle Sijtsema, Alan Thomas, Niels van de Ven, and Renée Zonneveld for the many helpful discussions about admiration while collaborating on two different projects looking at admiration and moral exemplars.

Some of this book draws on work that we co-authored with Amanda Cawston and Machteld Geuskens. We are grateful to them both for this collaboration.

Finally, we would like to thank our family and non-academic friends with whom we had many conversations on this topic including: Barnaby Archer, Jack Archer, John Archer, Laura Bennison, Rex Birchmore, Simon Frith, Clara Glynn, Michael Holiday, Catherine Matheson, David Matheson, Jenny McKay, Cressida McKay-Frith, Nick Tarlton, and Liam Young. A conversation Alfred had with John Archer, John Blake, Karen Brown, and Clara Glynn at the Mull of Kintyre proved particularly helpful at an important point in the writing process, and the book Karen sent him following this conversation played an important role in shaping our argument in Section 3 of Chapter 4. Thanks also to Macky the Cat for all of his emotional support.

Special thanks to Jenny McKay for spending an entire week proofreading and giving comments on this book before submission.

Finally, we would like to thank our partners Georgina Mills and Lucía Arcos Barroso for their love and support.

Earlier versions of parts of our arguments here have appeared in the following papers:

Archer, Alfred and Matheson, Benjamin (2019a) "When Artists Fall: Honoring and Admiring the Immoral". *Journal of the American Philosophical Association* 5 (2):246–265.

Archer, Alfred and Matheson, Benjamin (2019b). "Admiration and Education: What Should We Do with Immoral Intellectuals?" *Ethical Perspectives* 26 (1):5–32.

Archer, Alfred; Cawston, Amanda; Matheson, Benjamin; and Geuskens, Machteld (2020). "Celebrity, Democracy, and Epistemic Power". *Perspectives on Politics* 18 (1):27–42.

We thank Peeters publishers and Cambridge University Press for their permission to reuse this material.

A man may be admirable in many ways but a jerk in others.

Margaret Atwood, *Cat's Eye*

Introduction

In March 1977, a man was arrested in Los Angeles and charged with drugging and sexually assaulting a 13-year-old girl. The man pled not guilty to these charges, but eventually pled guilty to engaging in "unlawful sexual intercourse with a minor" in a plea bargain. But then, apparently because he believed the judge in charge of the case would renege on the plea bargain, the man fled the USA. Based on this information, it does not seem that this person merits admiration.

However, the man in question is the acclaimed film director Roman Polanski. He is widely regarded to be one of the world's greatest film directors. His film *Chinatown* has been judged to be the best film of all time (Pulver 2010), and he has received more than 80 international film awards. Audiences, actors, and critics admire his substantial contributions to cinema. For example, the actor Christoph Waltz said, "[Polanski] knows exactly what he wants and I admire that in a director. I admire Roman Polanski from A to Z" (Otto 2011).

This case highlights an ethical puzzle: Polanski has acted wrongly, yet he has also made many excellent contributions to the arts.[1] In light of his wrongdoing, should you still honour and admire him? Or should you instead blame and shun him? What exactly should your response to Polanski be?

Polanski's case is not unique. The #metoo movement has highlighted many other cases like Polanski's: cases of actors, producers, and musicians who have both acted immorally and created great art. In 2017, the comedian Louis CK acknowledged that he acted wrongly by masturbating in front of junior colleagues. In 2018, the actor and comedian Bill Cosby was convicted of three counts of aggravated sexual assault against Andrea Constand. In 2019, the singer R. Kelly was arrested and charged with various crimes, including "kidnapping, forced labor, child sexual exploitation and child pornography production and obstruction of justice" (Kaufman 2020).

DOI: 10.4324/9780367810153

In 2020, the producer Harvey Weinstein was sentenced to 20 years for a first-degree criminal sex act and three years for third-degree rape (Aratani and Pilkington 2020).

While there are many recent cases that have grabbed attention, this is not a recent phenomenon. The history of art features many artists who have done terrible things alongside creating excellent work. Richard Wagner was noted anti-Semite (Lee 1999). Pablo Picasso was a misogynist (Lee 2017). Paul Gauguin abused his wife (Hill 2001), abandoned his family to live in Tahiti, and then had three marriages to teenage girls, infecting each of them with syphilis (Bedworth 2018). We think that most people will have admired an artist – such as a musician, painter, actor, or a director – who has also done something immoral. So, even if you find yourself disagreeing with our judgements about a particular person being admirable or being immoral, we are sure that you will be able find a personal example to work with.

This phenomenon is not restricted to the arts. There are many examples of politicians, athletes, and intellectuals who have achieved great things and yet are (or were) immoral. For example, Winston Churchill is widely honoured and admired in the UK for playing an important role in helping to bring about victory for the Allied powers in the Second World War. In 2002, Churchill was voted "The Greatest Briton of All Time" in a British television poll (BBC News 2002). Likewise, Charles Krauthammer (1999), writing at the end of the twentieth century in *The Washington Post*, claimed Churchill was the "Person of the Century". However, Ross Greer (2019), a Member of the Scottish Parliament, says that Churchill was "a white supremacist mass murderer". Not only did Churchill hold many reprehensible views on race (Attar 2010: 9), he is also thought to have played a pivotal role in bringing about the 1943 Bengali famine which killed an estimated 1.5–3 million people (Mukerjee 2010: 131). The esteemed medical scientist Hans Asperger, who was once considered a hero by many people with autism, has been found to have been complicit in Nazi eugenicist policies (Sheffer 2018). The philosopher Martin Heidegger is responsible for significant works in the area of phenomenology. Not only has Heidegger been found to have held anti-Semitic views, but some have also argued that anti-Semitism is in fact a feature of his work (Oltermann 2014). And the widely honoured and admired footballer Cristiano Ronaldo has accepted a fine for tax evasion (Binnie 2019).

We therefore have a general ethical puzzle: what should the response be to those who have done both excellent things and immoral things? Should you honour and admire? Should you blame and shun them? Given that they have achieved great things, there are reasons to admire them. But given that they are also immoral, there are also reasons to blame and shun them. What, then, should you do? There is no obvious winner in this competition of reasons. This problem is especially pressing because, despite some efforts to change our practices of honouring and admiring inspired by the #metoo movement, we still have a culture in which people are regularly honoured and admired for their contributions to art, politics, science, philosophy, and sports without regard for the fact they have also done immoral things. For example, Polanski has received many awards and honours. Churchill has been honoured on British money, in statues, and in films about his life. All manner of immoral people – such as slave traders, colonialists, and the like – are depicted in statues around the world. And more informally, we honour immoral intellectuals by citing and using their work. Are these instances of honour and admiration unfitting or inappropriate? Should these statues be pulled down and these honours revoked?

The first two chapters of this book investigate the nature of honour and admiration in order to provide a guide to figuring out whether you have an instance of this ethical puzzle. In Chapter 1, we outline what we take honouring to be, what we take the connection between honouring and admiration to be, and what we take admiration to be. Among other things, we argue that honouring typically picks out its target as someone we ought to admire, and that admiration is fitting for those who have done something excellent. You might wonder whether a person's immorality precludes them also being admirable. If an immoral person cannot also be admirable, then there seems to be a simple answer to the ethical puzzle: the immoral should not be admired because they are not admirable. In Chapter 2, we take up this question. While we outline ways a person's immorality can affect their admirability, we argue that a person can be both immoral and admirable. So, you cannot simply avoid the puzzle at the heart of this book by holding that the admirability is incompatible with immorality. The ethical puzzle that we seek to respond to arises precisely because a person can be both admirable *and* immoral. Sometimes there are reasons to honour and admire a person *and* reasons to blame and shun that person.

While we think there is no immediately obvious correct response to this question, popular discussion about these questions highlights two general ways of responding to this puzzle. The first is that we should *do nothing* and maintain the status quo of honouring and admiring the immoral in the ways we already do. These people are admirable, so we should continue honouring and admiring them. This approach suggests that our honour and admiration practices are fine as they are and, hence, we have no need to change anything about who and how we honour and admire. This approach might seem especially objectionable in light of the #metoo movement, as many of its proponents called for those accused to cease being honoured. The second approach, which might seem inspired by the #metoo movement, is that we should *abandon* admiration of these immoral figures. These people have done terrible things, so they should not be honoured and admired. This approach suggests we have broken honour and admiration practices and that those who behave immorally should never be honoured and admired. This approach might seem like a form of so-called cancel culture. While our discussion does have implications for the debates about #metoo and cancel culture, the focus of the book will not be on these topics. There are two reasons. First, it does not seem that supporting the #metoo movement commits you to abandoning admiration in all or most cases. Second, it is not always clear what "cancelling" amounts to. Even so, sometimes what we count as "abandoning admiration" may qualify as "cancelling". If so, then our argument can be understood as this: cancelling is not a good general policy, but it is sometimes appropriate to cancel. We return to these wider cultural questions at the end of the book. Our focus until then is on the ethical puzzle of how to respond to admirable yet immoral people.

Once you have a clear instance of this puzzle, you have to turn to the ethics of admiration to figure out how you should respond to them. In Chapter 3, we outline a number of reasons against honouring and admiring the immoral. And in Chapter 4, we outline a number of reasons in favour of honouring and admiring the immoral. While the main focus of both of these chapters is on identifying factors that affect the appropriateness of honouring and admiring the immoral, both chapters reveal along the way that the *do-nothing* and the *abandoning-admiration* approaches are both unacceptable as general policies. Because both chapters argue that the only general reasons for and against honouring and admiring the immoral are defeasible ones (i.e. reasons that can be defeated or overridden by other reasons), these reasons cannot justify the above two general policies. This leaves open that sometimes it is appropriate to either do nothing and continue honouring and admiring an immoral person or abandon admiration and cease honouring and admiring an immoral person. Of course, sometimes neither approach will be an appropriate response to an immoral person.

In Chapter 5, we outline three other approaches when doing nothing and abandoning are off the table. Before outlining these approaches, we suggest that doing nothing and abandoning cannot constitute adequate general policies because they both manifest the vice of globalism – that is, they encourage or manifest the tendency to reduce a person to a particular feature, such as their admirable or immoral features. The further approaches, then, aim to avoid encouraging or manifesting this vice. The first two approaches we consider involve focused admiration. The first holds that we should aim to focus our honour and admiration on an immoral person's admirable traits and achievements (rather than letting admiration spread to all of the person's traits). The second holds we should aim to focus our honour and admiration only on the person's achievements. In other words, we should separate the achievement from the person and just focus on the achievement. The third holds that we should embrace the ambiguity that immoral yet admirable people force us into. Just as we suggest that focused admiration becomes an option once doing nothing and abandoning admiration are off the table, we suggest that achievement-focused admiration becomes an option once it is no longer acceptable to focus on the immoral person at all. Ambiguity, then, is in effect a kind of last-ditch option: we have strong reasons to honour and admire an immoral person (in some way) and yet we cannot easily avoid the moral dangers with doing so; we should instead try to mitigate those dangers by using our honour and admiration as a kind of educational experience about human nature, excellence, and immorality.

****

Our aim in this book is to provide the reader with a guide for responding to this important and complex ethical issue. We believe that philosophy works best when it provides people with a guide for helping them think through difficult issues rather than attempting to provide definitive answers to those questions. This kind of approach is summarized by Kwame Anthony Appiah:

> Philosophers contribute to public discussions of moral and political life, I believe, not by telling you what to think but by providing an assortment of concepts and theories you can use

to decide what to think for yourself. [...] I'm hoping to start conversations not to end them.

(2018: xiii)

Like Appiah, our aim is to provide resources to help the reader think these ethical issues through for themselves and to start conversations rather than to end them. We therefore do not aim to provide a definitive solution to the ethical puzzle of how we should respond to admirable yet immoral people. While we do not argue directly for this approach, we hope that this book serves as a kind of argument in its favour. Whether or not we are successful in any of our aims is something we leave for you, the reader, to judge.

Note

1   For ease of reference, we will sometimes refer to people who have acted wrongly or immorally as being "immoral". We do not mean that such people are thoroughly immoral. Rather, we just mean that they have done something immoral or have an immoral trait. Likewise, when we say someone has done something excellent in art, sport, politics, science, philosophy, or elsewhere, we will say that they are excellent artists, athletes, politicians, scientists, philosophers, even though we do not necessarily mean they are thoroughly excellent in these areas.

1 Honour and Admiration

What is it to honour? What is the connection between honouring and admiration? What is admiration? This chapter provides an answer to each of these questions. We argue that while honouring has several emotional bases, it functions to pick out its target as someone others ought to admire. Whether honouring is fitting, then, depends on whether admiration is fitting. We then outline some basic features of admiration. In particular, we claim it assesses its target as extraordinarily excellent, it can take on multiple objects (e.g. we can admire people, traits of people, nature, or objects), and that admiration need not involve a desire to emulate the target but can simply be a desire to promote the admired values in the object of admiration. It ends by arguing that we can morally evaluate feelings of admiration and we can perhaps even have duties to admire or not to admire.

1 The Nature of Honouring

We honour people in various ways: by giving them an award, by putting their face on a coin, by creating a statue of them and installing it in a prominent place, or by giving that person an important and prominent role (such as hosting a prestigious award ceremony). We may also honour a person by enjoying their work and by recommending their work to others (both in conversation and in academic research). Each honours a person because the object, process, role, or activity draw *positive attention* to that person. Due to space and attention constraints, the fact we could have drawn positive attention to someone else suggests that there is something special about the person towards whom we have drawn positive attention. Thus, in honouring that person, we send the message that the person is worth honouring.

DOI: 10.4324/9780367810153-1

There are different emotional bases for honouring. We might create a statue of a great political leader out of *gratitude* for that leader. For example, in the congressional record of the US Senate of a discussion of a statue of Winston Churchill that was placed in Washington D.C. outside the British Embassy it was said that the statue was "erected in eternal gratitude to Winston Churchill" for his role in defeating the Nazis during the Second World War (Brown Harris 1965: 2190). We might also honour someone out of *respect* and *admiration* for them. For example, when the Hollywood Foreign Press Association gave Oprah Winfrey a lifetime achievement award, HFPA President Meher Tatna called Winfrey "one of the most respected and admired figures today" (Bahiana 2017).

What does it mean to say an award or a statue or a role *expresses* an emotion? Given that such things lack emotions themselves – for example, a statue does not feel gratitude – it initially appears to be a convenient way of saying, for example, that the award-giver feels the emotion and they are giving the award as a way to show that they feel admiration for the awardee. There are two problems with this understanding. First, honours are often given by groups (such as a committee or nation), and, even if members of the group feel the relevant emotions, it need not be the case that the group as a whole feels those emotions. We may hold that groups simply cannot have emotions. Or we may hold that what emotions the group has isn't determined by what emotions most people in the group have.[1] Second, both individuals and groups can honour a person without feeling gratitude, respect, or admiration. For example, a scholar might cite another scholar out of duty without feeling respect, gratitude, or admiration.

However, when we honour a person, this does something. While honours can sometimes express gratitude, respect, and admiration of the person or group doing the honouring, we think that honours (given without qualification) will typically *pick out its target as worthy of admiration* – that is, as being admirable, as someone others have reason to or ought to admire. We think this is true regardless of what the honourers (those giving the honour) think or feel. As we have said, honouring takes up valuable resources, such as space and attention. Because it takes up such resources (as well as material resources), it communicates something about the person being honoured. It communicates that they are worthy of taking up our space and attention, of taking up these valuable and limited resources. And if they are worthy of this, then they must be someone for whom these are fitting reactions. Even if you just build a statue out of gratitude or just cite a person out of respect, you are still saying that this honour is a fitting response to this person. Statues make this particularly clear: when a person is put on a pedestal, they are elevated above others and so marked out in a positive way. If others want to receive such gratitude and respect and perhaps even adulation and adoration, then they should try to be like the person by also doing something great. In other words, in honouring a person it is usually being communicated that this person is admirable and that others therefore have reason to admire the person being honoured. (We say 'usually' because there may be ways to communicate that although someone is being honoured, they should not be admired. We return to this point later in the book.) While honouring often communicates more than just whether someone ought to be admired (e.g. it may also communicate that respect or gratitude are fitting responses), we will focus on just this particular meaning of honouring in what follows. Given that honours pick someone out as admirable – and can be said to express admiration in doing so – when a person is honoured this can be understood as saying that the honoured person is a fitting target of admiration.

2 Fittingness

Fittingness is a technical term used by philosophers to identify a relation between an emotion and the world. On the dominant view of fittingness, an emotion fits its targets if and only if it accurately represents the world (D'Arms and Jacobson 2000).[2] Suppose you feel fear. Your feelings of fear are fitting if and only if they are responding to something that is actually fearsome. If you felt fear upon seeing a dangerous bear, you would not be mistaken for doing so. However, if you felt fear because you mistook a bush for a bear, then you would be mistaken for doing so, as bushes are normally not dangerous. The idea is that our emotions have an implicit evaluation of a feature of the world, and this evaluation can be correct or incorrect depending on what the world is actually like. An emotion that has a correct evaluation, such as your fear of the bear, is fitting. An emotion that has an incorrect evaluation, such as your fear of the bush, is unfitting.

But just because an emotion is fitting does not mean that it is *all-things-considered* appropriate to feel that emotion (D'Arms and Jacobson 2000: 71–72). Fittingness is just one among many reasons that we might have for feeling an emotion. When an emotion is all-things-considered appropriate, the so-called balance of reasons speaks in favour of feeling this emotion. That is, given all the reasons there might be for and against feeling an emotion at a particular time, the reasons to feel the emotion win out. To see how fittingness and all-things-considered appropriateness come apart, consider the bear example again.

As we said, it is fitting to feel fear about the bear because the bear is a threat to your safety. By feeling fear about the bear, you are accurately evaluating the bear as a threat to your safety. While such a feeling may represent the world accurately – the bear is indeed a threat to your safety – feeling fear might cause you to startle the bear and lead to it attacking you. So even though fear is fitting, there is a prudential reason not to feel fear. This prudential reason (that it is better for you if you do not feel fear in this situation) plausibly overrides the fittingness reason to feel fear. So, feeling fear is not all-things-considered appropriate in this situation. Because the reason that fittingness gives to feel an emotion can be defeated by other reasons, fittingness only provides a defeasible or *pro tanto* reason to feel an emotion. In other words, fittingness is not sufficient for all-things-considered appropriateness.

Let us now apply these points about fittingness and all-things-considered appropriateness to admiration and honour. A person may be admirable – and so admiration for them is fitting – and yet it is not all-things-considered appropriate to admire them. So even though a person is admirable, the strength of the reasons to admire them can be overridden or defeated by reasons against admiring them. Perhaps your hero would feel very sad if you admired them; if so, then you plausibly have decisive reason not to admire them. The same is true with honouring, even though honouring is not itself an emotion but rather an activity. We can distinguish between a person being a fitting target of honour and it being all-things-considered appropriate to honour a person. Someone might think you were mocking them if you honoured them. If so, then you plausibly have decisive reasons not to honour them even though it is fitting to honour them. So, just because a person is a fitting target of an honour does not mean that you ought to honour them. There are further reasons – including moral, epistemic, and prudential reasons – that come into play in determining whether anyone should actually honour them.

Note also that just because an emotion is all-things-considered inappropriate in a particular situation we need not have a duty not to feel it. For instance, it may be all-things-considered inappropriate to feel fear when confronted with a bear, but, if you cannot suppress your fear, then it is plausible that you do not have a duty not to feel fear. After all, it is common to think we cannot have a duty or requirement to act in a particular way if we lack the power to act that way.[3] Likewise, it seems we cannot have a duty to feel or not to feel a particular feeling if we lack control over our feelings. It remains, though, that it is all-things-considered inappropriate. The balance of reasons may speak against feeling fear, even though your fear accurately represents a feature of the world, and you cannot help but feel fear in this particular situation. The same may be true when an emotion is all-things-considered appropriate: we may lack a duty to feel because we cannot bring about what it is all-things-considered appropriate to feel. Of course, when you have reasons for and against something, you may at some point get a duty to do or not do that thing.

Importantly, whether honour or admiration is fitting does not depend on whether it is public or private. Fittingness is just about getting the world right. It does not tell you what you ought to do, all-things-considered. But, as we will see later in more detail, whether honour and admiration are all-things-considered appropriate will often affect *how* you ought to honour and admire. Sometimes private admiration will be appropriate when public admiration is not, for example.

3 The Nature of Admiration

Whether admiration is fitting depends on what kind of evaluation is part of admiring and what the object of admiration is. After answering these questions about the nature of admiration, we look at a further component of admiration – namely, its action tendencies. Note two things.

First, we will not endorse any particular theory of emotions in this book. Instead, we will focus on an account of the admiration itself and on the aspects that are most relevant for our purposes.[4] Second, there are other aspects to admiration's nature that we will raise in later chapters as they become relevant. We provide this basic account here so that you have an initial understanding of the emotion we are investigating.

3.1 Evaluation

Admiration involves a positive evaluation of its object. For example, Aaron Ben-Ze'ev writes that admiration involves "a highly positive evaluation of someone" (2000: 56). Likewise, William Lyons says that admiration involves "an evaluation of [its] object which can be classed as a pro-evaluation or approval" (1980: 90). It is hard to challenge this claim about admiration. It does not seem that a feeling that lacked some sort of positive evaluation could plausibly count as admiration.

However, a positive evaluation is not distinctive of admiration. Adoration, respect, and gratitude also involve a positive evaluation. Admiration must therefore involve more than just a positive evaluation. Many claim that admiration also involves a kind of *wonder* (Smith [1759] 2007: I.i.4.3; Darwin [1872] 1998: 269; Schindler et al. 2013). Sophie Grace Chappell claims that admiration is "the 'Wow!' – response" (2019: 12). While Adam Smith says that admiration is "Approbation heightened by wonder and surprise" (1759/2007: I.i.4.3).

There may be other aspects to admiration's evaluative component. One suggestion is that admiring something involves viewing it as possessing value that is *rare* (Forrester 1982: 102). Another is that admiration involves a judgement of the object's *superiority in* relation to the subject (Schindler et al. 2013: 89; Chappell 2019: 15; Kauppinen 2019). Admiration has also been claimed to involve the judgement that the object being admired is *extraordinary* or even *miraculous* (Chappell 2019: 15). Drawing several of these suggestions together, our view is that admiration evaluates its target as being excellent and worthy of positive wonder.[5] So, admiration is fitting when these evaluations are correct. What, then, is the target of admiration?

3.2 Intentional Object

Unlike moods, emotions are *about* something. For example, we dislike *someone*, we are upset *that our team didn't win*, we enjoyed *the film*, and so on. The thing that emotions are about is their intentional object. But many emotions are about more than one thing – that is, they seemingly have multiple intentional objects. For example, we feel indignant *at someone* for *doing something*. In other words, while our indignation is targeted at a particular person, it is targeted at them because of something that they have done. We can distinguish two intentional objects for indignation – namely, a *particular* object and a *formal* object (Scarantino and de Sousa 2018; Kauppinen 2019). With indignation, the particular object is the person – that is, the particular person who has done something to be a fitting target of our indignation, while the formal object is what they have done to be a fitting target of our indignation. Indignation thus has a dual intentional object – one is the person towards whom we feel indignation and the other is the reason we have for feeling indignation towards them. It is an emotion's formal object that determines whether the emotion is fitting. If you felt indignation at a person who had not wronged you, you would be feeling unfitting indignation: it would inaccurately represent the person as having wronged you.

With respect to admiration, there is disagreement about which particular and formal objects it can have. There is widespread agreement that we can admire particular people – that is, that a person can be the particular object of admiration. However, Antti Kaupinnen (2019) claims that only people can be admired. Others instead hold that not only people can be fitting targets of admiration. Emily Brady (2013: 44) holds that we can admire natural events. Amanda Cawston (2019) claims we can admire animals. Chappell (2019: 13) claims that we can also admire qualities, relations, comic timing, positions, virtues, and actions, among other things. And Vanessa Wills (2019) argues that we can admire social groups such as the Paris Commune. While the ethical puzzle at the heart of this book involves person-focused admiration, we will also discuss object-focused admiration – such as admiration for a painting or for a scientific achievement. So, we assume pluralism about admiration's particular object.[6]

There is also disagreement about the formal objects that admiration can have. While many hold that admiration can be fitting because of a person's character traits, attitudes, actions, and achievements, some hold that admiration involves a *global* evaluation – for example, it involves holding that a person is (in some way) a purely admirable person and so lacks any non-admirable qualities. We discuss and reject this view in the next chapter. For the moment, we will assume pluralism about admiration's formal object too. On this view, a person is a fitting target of admiration only if they have acted excellently in some way, created an excellent object, or if they possess some excellent trait. An object is a fitting target of admiration only if it is excellent in some way.

3.3 Action Tendencies

An important part of experiencing an emotion is how that emotion motivates you to act – that is, what action tendencies that emotion has. When it comes to evaluating that emotion – in particular, in assessing what reasons you have against feeling an emotion – we need to know what action tendencies it has. While you might be making no factual error in feeling an emotion, you might make a moral error in doing so because it is going to motivate you to act in a particular way. What, then, are the action tendencies of admiration?

One popular view is that admiration motivates you to emulate the person you admire. For example, Linda Zagzebski (2017: 43) claims that admiring someone "gives rise to the motive to emulate the admired person in the way she is admired". Similarly, Mark Schroeder (2010: 42) claims that admiration "is the kind of state to motivate you to emulate the people you admire, insofar as you are able". It is important to make clear what the claim that admiration involves emulation amounts to. According to Zagzebski (2017), admiration typically gives rise to a defeasible desire to emulate the person we admire *in the way* that they are admired. If you admire a person for their courage, then this will give rise to a desire to become courageous yourself. The desire to emulate is therefore a desire to possess for yourself the features you admire in the other person. Zagzebski stresses that admiration is only likely to give rise to a desire to emulate when emulation is possible.[7,8]

Another view is that admiration involves a desire to promote the admired values in the object of admiration (Archer 2019). A virtue of this view is that it accommodates not only cases in which admiration leads to a desire to emulate but also other common instances of admiration that do not lead to such a desire. For example, John Skorupski claims that he can "admire the ease and grace of an athlete or violinist, the dedication of a scientist, the vision and courage of a politician, without desiring to emulate them" (2010: 288). This seems true. You can admire a footballer for their skills without desiring to gain those skills. Indeed, admiration may also have other action tendencies, such as applause (Smith 1759/2007 Ch.4 Section 1), enhancing the reputation and praising the object of admiration (Algoe and Haidt 2009), and deference to the admired (Velleman 2009: 42). This view can explain why people sometimes have desires to emulate, praise, or applaud the target of admiration. These are different ways that people can promote the admired values in the object of admiration.

4 Responsibility and Moral Evaluation

It is essential to our view that it is possible to have moral reasons against feeling admiration – that is, it is appropriate to subject our feelings of admiration to a particular kind of moral evaluation.

We also want our view to be compatible with people sometimes having a duty not to admire. If people cannot have duties not to admire, then we cannot say this. Some might be sceptical of both claims for a similar reason – namely, that we seem to lack control over our emotions.

Immanuel Kant (1996: 161) provides the following argument along these lines against the possibility of a duty to love: "Love is a matter of feeling, not of willing, and I cannot love because I will to, still less because I ought to (I cannot be constrained to love); so a duty to love is an absurdity". Similarly, Richard Taylor (1970: 252) claims that "Love and compassion are passions, not actions, are therefore subject to no terms of duties or moral obligations". These points can be adapted to become arguments against duties to admire or not to admire. Because admiration is also a matter of feeling or passion, it might also be thought to be something we cannot have a duty to feel. Similarly, it might be thought that love and admiration cannot even be morally evaluated because they are feelings we do not control.

Even if these lines of argument were sound, it would not undermine all our later claims – for example, that you sometimes have moral reasons (and sometimes even a duty) not to publicly admire or honour the immoral. Even if you accept that you cannot control your feelings of admiration, it is clear that you can control your expressions of admiration. People do this with other emotions. For example, a person feels angry at their teacher's questionable methods, but yet they can avoid showing any outward signs of anger. A person may feel very sad and yet appear very happy. There is no good reason that people cannot exhibit such control with admiration too. It is also clear that when people honour is under their control. It sometimes involves expressions of admiration and sometimes may not. Either way, these things can be controlled.

This line of argument is not sound, however, as there are different ways you can control your feelings.[9] First, you can have developmental control – that is, you can develop yourself so that you respond to the same stimuli with different emotions. Psychologists call this response modulation. Some people go to anger management classes in order to stop getting so angry at certain things. You can also come to care and appreciate your friends and family more by paying them greater attention, by reciprocating the kind things they have done for you, and so on. This kind of control is indirect because you do not change your emotions and attitudes immediately, but rather through a process of developing your character. Second, you can give yourself reasons to have or not to have an emotion. Psychologists call this attentional deployment. For example, a boxer might imagine someone they hate in order to get sufficiently angry to fight their opponent. Third, you can reflect on the reasons why you are feeling a certain emotion, and this may give you reason to stop feeling the emotion. Psychologists call this cognitive reappraisal. Consider the mother-in-law who feels contempt for her daughter-in-law until she reflects on the reasons why she feels this way (Murdoch 1970: 17–18). On discovering that her contempt is rooted in jealousy, the mother-in-law reflects on this and begins to see the daughter-in-law in a different light and eventually comes to like her. In this case, the mother-in-law's reflection influences her emotional response to the daughter-in-law. Fourth, you can place yourself in situations or avoid situations that are likely to bring about the desired emotion. Psychologists call this situation management. For example, a couple who want to feel more in love might spend a romantic weekend together. Because you can have these various forms of control over your emotions, it makes sense to say that you can have duties to feel or not feel particular emotions.

Perhaps more importantly, even if you cannot have duties to feel or not to feel, you can still morally evaluate how you feel. You can still judge that your excitement at someone else's misfortune is morally bad even if you cannot control that feeling. You can judge that any actions that stem from unconscious biases, and those biases themselves, are morally bad. You can evaluate any character trait, including ones you have not exercised much, if any, control over having. Even if you do not have control over these things, they are still expressive of who *you* are. These evaluations still tell you about what kind of person you are, whether you are good, bad, or mixed. You might not have a duty to do anything to curtail your immoral excitement or your morally bad biases. But because they can still be evaluated as morally bad, you arguably still have moral reason to try to curtail them. Many things in life generate reasons but not duties. Still, we think that sometimes these reasons might generate duties.

5 Conclusion

This chapter has investigated the basics of honouring and admiring. We first argued that the function of honouring is to pick out someone as admirable. This allows that those who honour need not feel admiration for the object of an honour. Because honouring picks someone out as admirable, whether a particular honour is fitting depends on whether admiration is fitting. After explaining the concept of fittingness, we then gave an initial account of admiration. Finally, we argued that you can have duties to feel and not to feel and, even if you do not have such duties, your feelings can be morally evaluated and you can have moral reasons against feeling a particular way.

Notes

1 For various understandings of what group collective emotions are, see Gilbert (2002), Pettigrove and Parsons (2012), von Scheve and Ismer (2013), Stockdale (2013), and Archer and Matheson (2019c).
2 There are other views. Macnamara (2020), for example, identifies four types of fittingness. Fittingness is also used in different ways across different debates – for an overview, see Howard (2018). We set aside these other views in what follows.
3 This claim – that "ought implies can" – has received considerable scrutiny. For a small sample of the literature on this topic, see Sinnot-Armstrong (1984), Yaffe (1999), and Vranas (2018).
4 In doing so, we follow the kind of approach taken by Deonna et al. (2012: 10). While they focus on seven dimensions of shame – namely, phenomenology, intentional object, evaluative component, the developmental path of acquisition, typical eliciting situations, manifestation, and associated action tendencies – we focus on a narrower set given our different purposes.
5 This claim is compatible with leading accounts of the emotions. For example, judgementalists (e.g. Nussbaum 2001) could say that the evaluation involved in admiration is a belief or judgement. Perceptualists (e.g. Tappolet 2016) could understand the evaluation as a perception. Sentimentalists (e.g. D'Arms and Jacobson 2003) could either say that admiration is a natural emotion and so a positive feeling, or they could say it is a cognitive sharpening of a positive natural emotion. Attitudinalists (e.g. Deonna and Teroni 2015) could understand the evaluation as an attitude that the object of admiration is admirable. Note, though, that we will normally talk about our emotions representing the world. We take it that this way of talking can be translated into one's preferred view of the emotions.
6 See Archer (2019) for a defence of pluralism.
7 This leads Zagzebski (2017: 35–40) to restrict her claim to admiration for acquired excellences rather than natural talents. We will not examine this part of her view here.
8 The emulation view is supported by a number of psychological studies. See Algoe and Haidt (2009), Aquino et al. (2011), Cox (2010), Freeman et al. (2009), Immordino-Yang and Sylvan (2010), Landis et al. (2009), Schnall et al. (2010), Thrash and Elliot (2004), and van de Ven et al. (2019). It is worth noting that not all of the psychological evidence

speaks in favour of the emulation view. A study by Van de Ven et al. (2011) cast doubt on this connection, finding no statistically significant connection between admiration and a desire to emulate. Instead, they found that what they call benign envy was more likely to lead to such a desire. However, in later work, van de Ven (van de Ven 2017; van de Ven et al. 2019) did find a connection between admiration and a desire to emulate and conceded that the balance of evidence speaks in favour of this connection (van de Ven 2017: 197).

9 Some of these points are drawn from Liao (2006: 4). Some are drawn from the extensive psychological literature on the topic of *emotion regulation*, a term that refers to the ways in which people manage their emotions. See Gross (2015) for a helpful survey of this literature. See Archer and Mills (2019) and Liebow and Glazer (forthcoming) for philosophical work that engages with this literature.

2 Admirability and Immorality

Can someone be admirable despite being immoral? In other words, can the immoral be fitting targets of admiration? This question is of crucial importance for our project of providing an ethical guide to admiring the immoral. If the immoral can never be fitting targets of admiration, then the ethical question of whether or not we should honour and admire them will be virtually redundant.[1]

To show that this ethical question is not redundant, we will argue in Section 1 that the immoral can be admirable. We will argue for this by undermining arguments for admiration being a globalist emotion. On this view, admiration evaluates (i.e. takes as its formal object) the whole person. However, we will argue that people can be complex, have both good and bad traits, and still be admirable.

But how exactly can the immoral be admirable? Can they be admirable *for* being immoral? Or are they just admirable *despite* being immoral? In Section 2, we will investigate the admirable immorality debate to identify ways that the immoral can be admirable. We argue that the immoral may be admirable despite being immoral but are never admirable for their immorality. But just because the immoral can be admirable despite being immoral, this does not mean that immorality never affects admirability. In Sections 3–5, we outline three ways a person's immorality can affect whether they are a fitting target of admiration. The first involves their immorality giving us evidence that they did not do something admirable in the first place. The second involves a person's immorality affecting the (aesthetic) value of their work. The third involves their later immorality undermining their earlier admirability.

DOI: 10.4324/9780367810153-2

1 Globalism

1.1 Globalism about Admiration

Globalist emotions take the "whole person" as both the particular and formal object. Shame is often invoked as a paradigm example. For example, Bernard Williams writes that, "in the experience of shame, one's *whole being* seems diminished or lessened. In my experience of shame, the other sees *all of me* and all through me" (1993: 89; our emphasis). And Martha Nussbaum writes that "Whereas shame focuses on defect or imperfection, and thus on *some aspect of the very being of the person* who feels it, guilt focuses on an action (or a wish to act), but *need not extend to the entirety of the agent*, seeing the agent as utterly inadequate" (2004: 207; our emphasis). The "whole person" in these contexts is understood psychologically such that it includes all of the person's beliefs, desires, values, traits, cares, and commitments.

A globalist view of admiration holds that whether a person is a fitting target of admiration depends on an evaluation of the whole person. On this view, when you admire a person, you can only fittingly admire them for *being an admirable person*. The formal object of your admiration is the person and not some feature of the admired person (such as their artistic talent or moral virtue).[2] If someone's immorality means that an overall positive evaluation of the person is not possible, then, according to a globalist view of admiration, they cannot be a fitting target of admiration. On some conceptions of globalism (e.g. Bell 2011), this does not rule out the possibility that someone may be both admirable and immoral. You might still be able to have an overall positive evaluation of a person even though they are immoral, because their admirable traits and actions might outweigh or be more important than their immoral traits and actions. However, it does mean that you must always take someone's immorality into account when evaluating whether they are a fitting target of admiration. On stronger views of globalism, admirability is incompatible with immorality.[3] The ethical puzzle at the heart of this book would then be easily resolved: you must simply work out whether or not a person is admirable overall in order to know whether or not you should honour and admire them.

While there are different accounts of the relevant global evaluation (e.g. Doris 2003; Bell 2011), we will not investigate the differences between these accounts here (though these accounts will be relevant to our discussion in Chapter 5). Rather, we will argue that there is no good reason to think that admiration is globalist in the first place.

As we alluded to in the previous chapter, our admiration practices do not offer support for globalism about admiration. While people are sometimes admired for the kind of person they are in general (e.g. they are admired for all their attitudes), people are also admired for what they do (e.g. a person is admirable for being patient with their child), for the kind of person they are at specific times (e.g. we admire a person for simply being disposed to be patient with children). Rather than rest our case against admiration being globalist on these examples, we will instead argue against globalism by undercutting the two best reasons for thinking that admiration is globalist. These reasons are based on two arguments that have been given in favour of other emotions being globalist.

1.2 The Permeation Argument

Michelle Mason claims that "contempt permeates one's interactions with the person who is its object in a way that resentment typically does not" (2003: 249). Mason's point is that when we have contempt for someone, this colours all of our interactions with them. Suppose you feel contempt for your slobby roommate. According to Mason, feeling contempt for your roommate will lead to this description of them becoming salient in all of your interactions with them. This is not the case with resentment, according to Mason. You can apparently resent the fact that a colleague's ambition led them to use underhanded tactics to get a promotion over you without letting that colour all of your interactions with them. Because contempt permeates and so implies a global evaluation of the person, contempt is globalist.

A similar argument could be made for admiration being a globalist emotion. Suppose you find out your short-tempered colleague gives up a significant amount of their spare time helping sick children. This may well lead to you feel admiration for them. It is a familiar experience that feelings of admiration such as this one can cast a positive light on the other aspects of the person being admired. You may begin to find their temper less objectionable, more an idiosyncrasy than a character flaw. You may start to wonder if their lack of patience for timewasters is somehow connected to their commitment to dedicating their spare time to those in need. This may be a form of the halo effect, the unconscious process through which seeing a person in a positive light leads us to continue to see them in that light. This results in a positive judgement about a person's abilities in one area leading to more positive judgements of that person in other, unrelated areas (Gräf and Unkelbach 2016).

It seems clear that admiration for one aspect of a person can spread to our evaluation of other aspects.

However, there is a big gap between saying that admiration has a tendency to spread and saying that it typically permeates all of our interactions with that person. Admiration does often spread from one aspect of a person to another, and this may on occasion permeate all of your interactions with that person. However, it is also the case that you can admire someone without that admiration permeating all of your interactions with that person. You may admire a friend's talent as a chef, but this may make no difference to how you view them when you are playing chess together. While there are cases of admiration permeating, these do not show that admiration typically permeates. Rather than having a permeating quality, admiration more plausibly has a *spreading tendency*: we admire one aspect of a person but sometimes end up admiring – or even just looking favourably upon – other aspects of them. Your admiration for your chef friend might make you more understanding of their grumpiness without making you see them as a better chess player. A tendency to spread is not the same as a permeating quality, because permeation suggests it spreads across all interactions.

Moreover, the fact that admiration spreads from one part of a person to another does not tell us that it takes the whole person as its formal object. Paradigm non-globalist emotions also have the tendency to spread. For example, if you feel resentment towards someone who makes a derogatory comment about you, then you may start seeing other parts of their character in a new light. Similarly, if you feel guilty for letting down a friend, this may lead you to consider many different aspects of yourself in a new light. In both cases, though, this does not show that these emotions are globalist. The permeation argument therefore fails to establish that admiration is a globalist emotion.

1.3 The Action Tendencies Argument

One reason given for shame being a globalist emotion is that this is implied by its tendency to get us to hide ourselves or to reconstruct ourselves. Williams says that shame involves "not just the desire to hide, or to hide my face, but the desire to disappear, not to be there" (1993: 89) and that it also involves "attempts to reconstruct or improve oneself" (1993: 90). Because we seemingly react to our whole self being implicated when we feel shame, we apparently have reason to think that shame is a globalist emotion.

Do admiration's action tendencies speak in favour of it being globalist? As we discussed in Chapter 1, admiration is often associated with the action tendency of emulation (Zagzebski 2017). If admiration is globalist, then the whole person typically ought to be emulated. This might sometimes happen when we admire a person: we might find ourselves striving to emulate them and everything they do. For example, a graduate student who admires their supervisor might find themselves emulating not only their supervisor's philosophical style but also their way of speaking and dressing. But even if we assume that emulation is the action tendency of admiration (rather than the promotion of admired values), emulation of the whole person is not typical of admiration. First, recall Linda Zagzebski's words, "admiration for the admired person moves us to emulate the admired person *in the respect in which the person is admired*" (2017: 33; our emphasis). Second, as we discussed, Zagzebski's claim is supported by a range of psychological studies. Third, we think it is clear from our experiences of admiration that we do not typically try to emulate everything about the person we admire. In short, admiration's action tendencies actually give us reason to think that admiration is not globalist.

If admiration were a globalist emotion, then immorality would always be relevant to our assessment of a person's admirability. We would then have an easy solution to the ethical puzzle: assess the person and that will give us the fitting response to them and a guide to how to respond them. However, there is no good reason to think that admiration is a globalist emotion. It is therefore possible for a person to be immoral *and* admirable. Even though this is possible, it will be important to be clear on the ways that the immoral can be admirable and whether immorality can ever affect a person's admirability. In the next section, we will outline different ways an immoral person can be admirable and what the relationship between their admirability and their immorality can be. In the following three sections, we will consider ways that immorality can affect admirability.

2 Admirable Immorality

Can a person be admirable *for* being immoral – that is, can they be admirable *in virtue of* their immorality? Or are they just admirable *despite* their immorality? If the former is true, then people can be admirable for acting wrongly, possessing moral vices, and the like. If the latter is true, then people are not admirable for acting wrongly and possessing moral vices but acting wrongly and possessing moral vices need not preclude them being admirable; people may even be admirable for traits and actions closely related to their immoral ones.

Let us begin by considering some of the various ways in which people can be admirable. Someone may be *morally* admirable for displaying exemplary integrity. Alternatively, they might also be *aesthetically* admirable if they have created a magnificent artwork. Someone might be *epistemically* or *intellectually* admirable if they have achieved great things in philosophy, science, or mathematics. Just because we are admirable in one normative domain does not mean we are admirable in all normative domains. A person could be morally admirable, but not aesthetically admirable. For example, a moral hero might create bad art. And someone could be aesthetically admirable but not morally or intellectually admirable. For example, a great artist could do morally terrible things or have wacky views based on bad reasoning and insufficient evidence.

These different ways in which someone may be admirable highlight a feature of admiration we identified in Chapter 1: admiration is directed both to a particular person and to a property that is being attributed to that person. If you admire Polanski for his talent as a filmmaker, then your admiration is targeted both at Polanski and also to the property 'talented filmmaker' that you are ascribing to him. Polanski is the particular object of your admiration: he is the thing in the world towards which you are directing your admiration. Polanski's being *a talented filmmaker* is the formal object: it is this property or feature of Polanski that makes him a fitting target of admiration.

While it is possible for a person to be admirable in all these ways – that is, morally, aesthetically, and intellectually admirable – it is more common for someone to be admirable in only one of these ways. Indeed, it is even more common that a person is admirable in relation to a quite specific formal object – for example, being a talented scientist. Someone may be incredibly talented as a scientist but have very little artistic talent. This person would be a fitting target of admiration in relation to the formal object 'talented scientist' but not in relation to the formal object 'talented artist'. Determining whether admiration is fitting involves working out whether the person who is admired possesses the property in question and that this property at least merits positive evaluation.

We can now see the first way in which a person can be both admirable and immoral: they may be a fitting target of admiration in virtue of non-moral formal objects despite being immoral. Less technically, they may be admirable for aesthetic, intellectual, or athletic traits and achievements, even if they are immoral. This seems a plausible way to view an artist like Polanski. He is admirable in virtue of his aesthetic talents and achievements but not in virtue of his moral failures. In this case, the source of a person's admirability is different from what makes them immoral.

According to an influential line of argument, there can be a much closer connection between a person's admirability and their immorality. According to this view, the trait or action that makes one immoral may also be what makes one admirable. To support his claim that we have reasons to be grateful that we do not live in a world full of morally perfect people, Williams (1981) uses the (perhaps not historically accurate) example of the artist Paul Gauguin, who abandoned his family to go to Tahiti, where, according to Williams, he produced his best works of art. Williams (1981: 23) claims that Gauguin's treatment of his family is immoral but that "we have deep and persistent reasons to be grateful" that we live in a world in which such immorality exists. Michael Slote (1983) builds on Williams' discussion to argue that this kind of case demonstrates "admirable immorality".

By this Slote does not mean to defend the strong thesis that a trait or action can be admirable *in virtue of* being immoral. Rather, Slote is claiming that the same trait or action can be both admirable for non-moral reasons and immoral. To see the difference between these two views, consider again the case of Gauguin. On the strong version of the admirable immorality claim, Gauguin could be admirable *for* his immoral behaviour – for example, for abandoning his family. Slote claims (rightly, in our view) that this is implausible. On the moderate version of the admirable immorality view that Slote endorses, the same trait or action can ground a person's immorality and their admirability, but the person is not admirable for the trait or action as an immoral trait or action. For example, Slote (1983: 80) claims that we can admire Gauguin's single-minded pursuit of artistic excellence while at the same time judging that this trait causes him to act immorally. In this case, although we are not admiring the immorality itself, the traits we admire are inseparable from the immoral behaviour. Slote argues that this shows that morality is not overriding – that is, that moral reasons do not always trump non-moral reasons. Our interest is not in the overridingness thesis,[4] but rather Slote's account of how a person can be admirable despite being immoral.

So far we have considered two ways a person can be admirable for non-moral reasons despite being immoral. A third way a person can be admirable despite being immoral involves a person who is *morally* admirable despite being immoral. Examples of this kind of admirable immorality arise when we consider cases of conflict within morality, such as the following example:

> A father may deliberately mislead police about his son's where-abouts, even knowing that the son has committed a serious crime and even while acknowledging the validity of the local system of criminal justice. He may feel he mustn't let the police find his son, but must, instead, do everything in his power to help him get to a place of safety, even though he is also willing to admit that there can be no moral justification for what he is doing.
>
> (Slote 1983: 86)

While Slote (1983: 88) sees this as a case of a conflict between moral and non-moral concerns, another way of interpreting this case is to see it as a conflict between two different moral demands: the demand to protect one's child and the demand to respect a reasonable law that requires that those who have committed serious crimes be pun-ished. We might instead think it highlights that the ethics of care and the ethics of justice come into conflict (Curzer 2002: 229). Care for one's child speaks in favour of protecting the son while a respect for justice speaks against it. Or we might understand this as involv-ing what Troy Jollimore (2006) calls morally admirable immorality: the behaviour is both morally wrong and admirable from the moral point of view.[5] If we think that in this case the father has a duty to re-port the son to the police but that it would also be morally admirable for the father to get his son to safety instead, then we should accept that morally admirable immorality is possible.

There are other kinds of cases that fall into this third category of admirable immorality. This includes the so-called dirty hands case in which a person who has good moral reasons does something morally wrong, such as torturing someone to stop a bomb going off (Curzer 2002).[6] We do not think that many, if any, cases of admira-ble yet immoral people that we consider in this book will fall into this third category. We discuss these different ways of people being admirable despite being immoral so that it is clear what we think the claim that the immoral may also be admirable amounts to.

But what about the strong admirable immorality view? Perhaps people are sometimes admirable *because* they are immoral. That is, perhaps people are sometimes admirable in virtue of their immo-rality. This has not been true in any of the cases we have discussed so far. Even the father in Slote's example is not admirable in virtue of acting immorally: if he had not been doing something good for his son, he would not be admirable for his actions. The father does something that is both excellent and immoral: the father's action is excellent (and so admirable) under one description and immoral under another.

Could a person be admirable and immoral for a trait or action under the same description? This might seem possible because it is common for people to admire criminals and other immoral people for what they have done. For example, Bonnie Parker and Clyde Barrow who, together with other members of the Barrow Gang, _ conducted a high-profile series of bank robberies and murders in the United States between 1932 and 1934. Bonnie and Clyde gained a great deal of newspaper coverage and popularity. Jeff Guinn (2009: 3–4) describes them as "colourful young rebels" who "came to epitomise the edgy daydreams of the economically and socially downtrodden" and were "considered the epitome of scandalous glamour".

An initial point is that these cases can be interpreted in different ways. Perhaps people actually have a form of horrified fascination that has nothing to do with admiration. Or we might think that people admired Bonnie and Clyde's glamour *despite* their criminal deeds such that this is just one of three forms of admirable immorality we have identified above. Another possibility is that people admire Bonnie and Clyde for their criminality, but they do not judge their criminality to be immoral. This still leaves the possibility that some people admire them precisely because they judge their actions to be immoral.

Even if some people have a positive evaluation of immorality that means they admire some people in virtue of their immorality, we think that such admiration is unfitting. Consider a point from Marcia Baron (1986). If Gauguin's commitment to his art showed no bounds at all, such that he was willing to kill to obtain art supplies or murder his own children in the process of creating an artwork, then his commitment to his art would no longer be admirable. Some people might still admire this Gauguin, but we think those people would be mistaken to do so. Indeed, we think it is often the case that people are fascinated with immoral figures such as Bonnie and Clyde for features other than their immorality. Part of the puzzle that this book is trying to answer stems from the fact that sometimes admiration for immoral people is fitting. While it is implausible that the immoral are ever fitting targets of admiration in virtue of their immorality, they can be admirable for traits and actions that are intimately related to their immorality. For example, we might fittingly admire Bonnie and Clyde's *daring* in engaging in their crime spree. But this does not mean they are admirable for *engaging in their crime spree.*

In short, while people can be admirable despite being immoral, and you might even admire them for traits or actions that are immoral under a different description (i.e. traits and actions that are closely connected to immorality), it is not fitting to admire people for their immorality. But while the immoral can also be admirable, it does not follow that immorality never affects admirability. In the rest of this chapter, we outline three ways that immorality can affect admirability.

3 Immorality as Evidence

Sometimes a person's immorality reveals to us that they have not done anything worthy of admiration. Consider the following example. The British entertainer and DJ, Sir Jimmy Savile, was widely honoured and admired for his public persona and philanthropy during his lifetime. After he died in 2011, police investigations revealed that he was one of the UK's worst sexual predators. Beyond his hundreds of victims (ranging from the very young to the very old), he used his charity work in various hospitals as *cover* for his heinous actions: he found many of his victims through this apparent philanthropic work. While Savile *appeared* admirable during his lifetime, he was not in fact admirable. The behaviour that seemed to be admirable was performed in the service of appalling acts of abuse. He was not actually a fitting target of any of the honours or any of the admiration that he often received. Indeed, many of his honours were revoked once the allegations came to light.

This suggests that a person's immorality can effectively cancel out their admirability. Savile would have been admirable for his charity work if it did not have the purpose of facilitating his heinous acts of abuse. In Savile's case, we mistakenly believed he was admirable for his charity work because we did not realize that work was a cover for his predatory behaviour. Savile's case reveals an epistemic connection between admirability and immorality: a person's immorality may reveal that they were not in fact admirable all along. In this case, it tells us about the true nature of their actions. Savile's acts were not really charitable acts. So, immorality can sometimes be evidence that a person is not admirable.

4 Immoral Art

While this book concerns more than just immoral artists, it is worth mentioning a potential way that an artist's immorality can affect their admirability. A longstanding debate in aesthetics concerns whether immoral artworks are less aesthetically valuable – that is, less excellent – because they have immoral features. More recently, certain philosophers have argued that immorality in an artist's life can affect the aesthetic value of their work (e.g. Gaut 2007; Bartel 2019).

On Berys Gaut's (2007) *ethicism* an artwork can be immoral if it endorses immoral attitudes. If an artwork is immoral, then it may (but importantly need not) lose aesthetic value. Endorsement requires more than mere depiction. We often enjoy art in which immorality is depicted, but in which the art itself does not endorse that immorality. In some art, though, it seems that the immoral attitudes are endorsed. The Nazi propaganda film *The Triumph of the Will* is often raised as an example of immoral art (e.g. Jacobson 1997). If an artwork endorses an immoral attitude held by the artist, then (according to ethicism) an artist's immorality can affect the aesthetic value of the work.

Christopher Bartel (2019) expands Gaut's ethicism. Bartel argues that sometimes artworks that contain no trace of an artist's immorality can still lose aesthetic value because of the artist's immorality. His main example is the work of Bill Cosby. Because Cosby's performance traded on an insincere depiction of his actual character, Cosby's work loses value as a result of the revelations that he sexually assaulted Andrea Constand (among other accusations of similar behaviour). Bartel argues that because we sometimes take artworks to be more aesthetically valuable because of an artist's life, we should also take artworks to be less aesthetically valuable because of an artist's life.

Bernard Wills and Jason Holt (2017) agree that *sometimes* an artist's immorality can affect the aesthetic value of their work. However, they hold that it is only in rare and exceptional cases that it does so. These are cases where an artist has lived what they depict in their work. They write:

> People who live their art are inviting judgments on their character and their art together, as they make no separation between the two. That Sade actually attempted the sadistic deeds described at such length in *Justine* and *120 Days of Sodom* kills his books for many people, for they then become not fantasy but an implicit apology for his own brutishness.
>
> (Wills and Holt 2017)

They argue that these kinds of artworks manifest a "cold calculating aspect", and this is why the artist's immorality is relevant to its aesthetic value. The aesthetic value of works that simply manifest "ordinary vices of passion" is not affected by the artist's immorality. Importantly, because they endorse autonomism (the view that aesthetic value is independent from moral value) with exceptions, they do not agree with Gaut and Bartel that mere endorsement of immoral attitudes in an artwork affects its aesthetic value.

Another view is that immorality in artworks can *increase* its aesthetic value. Daniel Jacobson (1997) argues that sometimes immorality in artwork increases aesthetic value, though he also holds that sometimes artworks gain aesthetic value because they endorse moral attitudes. It is unclear whether Jacobson would agree that an artist's real-life morality or immorality could affect the aesthetic value of their work. Still, we might extend his anti-theoretical view of aesthetic value such that an artist's real-life immorality could increase an artwork's aesthetic value. For example, the comedian Louis CK's masturbation jokes might be even funnier because they are connected to his real-life wrong of masturbating in front of junior colleagues.

If Jacobson (1997) holds that immoral artworks are aesthetically valuable *in virtue of* their immorality, then he is making a stronger claim than any of those involved in the admirable immorality debate – a point that Smuts (2013) and Paris (2018) both make. However, it is unclear that Jacobson is best understood as making this point. He claims at one point that certain immoral artworks provide a unique opportunity to understand the workings and allure of immorality, as well as avoiding dogmatism and offering an opportunity to see how others think (Jacobson 1997: 193). But this explanation for the aesthetic value of immoral artworks seems to imply they are valuable in virtue of their *insight into immorality*. This is importantly different from being valuable *for their immorality*. Of course, we perhaps cannot get that insight without the artwork being immoral, but the object of admiration is importantly different on our reading. We admire the insight, not the immorality itself. So, even on this view it is not an artist's immorality that increases aesthetic value, but rather a different feature of the work.

This is only a brief and simplified survey of a longstanding debate. We raise it not to settle it, but rather to note that there it is an open question whether an artist's immorality can decrease the value of their work. If immorality can decrease aesthetic value, then an artist could become less admirable because of their immorality. Indeed, it may well be that a person's immorality can undermine the value of their achievements in other areas. For example, an intellectual work might have less value because it is intimately connected to its creator's immorality.

5 Admirability over Time

Sometimes our heroes change. In certain kinds of cases, our heroes can stop being admirable (Archer and Matheson 2020). Consider Aung San Suu Kyi. She was given the Nobel Peace Prize in 1991 "for her non-violent struggle for democracy and human rights" (the Nobel Peace Prize 1991). More recently, however, she has faced moral scrutiny for not speaking out against war crimes (including genocide, ethnic cleansing, and mass rape) perpetrated by her country's military against the Rohingya people. We think that Suu Kyi has ceased being admirable. This does not mean she never was admirable. Rather, it means that her later actions have undermined her *continued* admirability. We could still think back to her earlier self and fittingly feel admiration at the kind of person she was (just as you could admire painting before it is ruined in a botched restoration), but she is not *now* a fitting target of admiration for her earlier traits and achievements.

We accept that there may be other ways to interpret this case (e.g. she has become a different person, or she was never really admirable in the first place). However, we think that cases in which people can change in the way we have described are possible. In this case, the person's later immorality in some sense defeats her earlier admirability. We discuss this case and other cases like this in more detail elsewhere, and we defend the view that admiration for actions is connected to ideals (Archer and Matheson 2020). The important point for our present discussion is that someone's later immorality can prevent them from remaining admirable for some earlier action. We think that this holds not just for moral behaviour. An artist, athlete, or intellectual could also in some cases cease being admirable. Importantly, the later behaviour that defeats admirability for earlier actions must be connected to the earlier actions. So, it is not just any later immorality will defeat admirability for earlier actions.[7]

6 Conclusion

We have reached the end of the first part of our guide into the ethical puzzle surrounding admirable yet immoral people. Our focus has been on the question of whether the immoral can be admirable, and we have argued that they can be. Even though there are ways immorality can undermine admirability, it remains the case that a person can be both immoral and admirable. When you are faced with what you think is an instance of this ethical puzzle – a person you admire who is also immoral – you must ask yourself whether the person is in fact both admirable and immoral. It might be that their immorality undermines their admirability, so you need to check that this is not the case. If so, then the puzzle is easily resolved: the person is not a fitting target of admiration, and so you should not honour and admire them.[8] If it is not the case, you can also ask yourself what the formal object of your admiration is. If you are admiring the person *for* their immorality, then we think your admiration is unfitting and you have another easy answer for what you should do. But recall an earlier point from Chapter 1: just because a person is a fitting target of admiration, it does not follow that you ought to admire them, because fittingness reasons can be defeated. So, even once you have established that a person is a fitting target of admiration, you still have questions to ask yourself. These are questions about the *ethics of honour and admiration*.

Notes

1 But not completely redundant, as there may be cases where we have instrumental reasons to admire the immoral even though they are not fitting targets of admiration. In such cases, the ethical issues would be about whether admiration is all-things-considered appropriate would remain.
2 Kauppinen (2019) defends what he calls a globalist view about admiration, but it is not globalist in the sense we have in mind. He holds that an emotion is globalist if it only takes the person as its particular object. This is therefore rather a person-only view of admiration. He holds a person's other traits are not relevant to whether admiration is fitting, but rather whether admiration is all-things-considered appropriate. On his view, then, a person may be admirable despite being immoral. However, the person's immorality might make it all-things-considered inappropriate to admire them.
3 Bell (2011) attributes this kind of view to Doris (2003).
4 Though see Archer (2014) for one of the author's views on overridingness.
5 Jollimore (2006) argues that there is room for cases of morally admirable immorality within several plausible moral theories.
6 This kind of case is in tension with the empirical evidence that suggests that torture is not an effective way of obtaining information (see, for example, Costanzo and Gerrity 2009).
7 For more on responsibility over time, see Matheson (2014, 2019a, 2019b) and Khoury and Matheson (2018).
8 In most cases anyway. It is possible for there to be reasons to honour and admire those who are not admirable. Suppose something really terrible will happen if you do not honour Jimmy Savile with a statue. Plausibly you should build a statue of Savile to avoid the really terrible thing happening. We take it that these are non-typical cases, and so typically you should not honour and admire people who are not admirable.

3 Reasons against Honouring and Admiring

A person can still be admirable even though they are immoral. Should you honour and admire them? Remember that fittingness is not sufficient for all-things-considered appropriateness, so the fact a person is admirable does not yet tell you whether you should honour and admire them. While you might not make a factual error in honouring and admiring the immoral, you might still make a *moral* one. To answer this question, then, you have to turn to the ethics of honour and admiration. In this chapter, we outline three general moral reasons against honouring and admiring the immoral. First, that it empowers the wrongdoer in various ways. Second, that it harms the victims. Third, that it perpetuates harmful ideologies and wrongdoing. We end by discussing how these reasons can vary in strength depending on the specifics of certain cases, and on who is doing the honouring and admiring, among other factors.

1 Empowering Perpetrators

The first reason against honouring and admiring the immoral is that it can empower them in various ways. First, it can contribute to their financial power. This is quite simply the power to pay for things. Second, it can give them epistemic power – that is, it can give them power over what people believe and over who can exert influence on people's beliefs (Archer et al. 2020).[1] Third, it can give them moral power – that is, power to influence people's moral judgements. We are most interested in the ability to influence people's judgements about whether what a person is doing is tolerable or acceptable, or even justifiable or excusable. Fourth, it can give affective power to the immoral – that is, it can give them power over what people feel and over who can exert influence on people's emotions.

Note that these different forms of power may overlap and interconnect. Affective power may increase a person's financial power,

DOI: 10.4324/9780367810153-3

epistemic power, and moral power. Likewise, moral power may increase a person's affective power, financial power, and epistemic power. We will identify a factor that supports each form of power. These factors will be important for our discussion in Section 4. In this section, we will focus on showing how one factor supports a particular form of power but note that the identified factors may also support other forms of power just as each form of power can support another. These factors may even be reasons against honouring and admiring in their own right, but we will focus on how they support these more general reasons.

1.1 Financial Power

One distinctive way you contribute to the financial power of the immoral when you honour and admire them is simply by drawing positive attention to them. Often having greater positive attention gives a person more opportunities. The person who gets hired is sometimes the person others have heard good things about. If an immoral person gets more work, then they will usually get more money and so more financial power. According to one study, being nominated for a best picture or best leading actor nomination for *The Oscars* increases weekly box office revenue by 200 percent (Deuchert et al. 2005: 164). The positive attention gained through such nominations is clearly quite profitable. By honouring and admiring a person, you may contribute to their financial power.

1.2 Epistemic Power

While there are many factors that contribute to epistemic power, one important factor is how epistemically credible you find them (Archer et al. 2020). Consider how many fans of Michael Jackson still deny the allegations against him despite significant evidence of his guilt. One explanation is that Jackson's fans might find him more epistemically credible than they ought to. Indeed, the director of *Leaving Neverland*, which documented his alleged abuse of two young boys, is reported to have said, "One can only compare [Jackson's fans] to religious fanatics" (Coscarelli 2019). Because of this, they are more likely to believe his denials of guilt while he was alive (and denials of guilt on his behalf after his death) than other people's accusations against him.

When you honour and admire a person, you are drawing positive attention to them. You are elevating them above others and as well as picking them out as people others ought to admire, you also pick them out as people others ought to listen to. One reason for this is that honour and admiration for them can spread in the perception of others. Because you draw positive attention to the person, it might seem you are picking them out as being overall admirable. If they are overall admirable, they may seem like someone people ought to listen to. When you give epistemic power to the immoral, you are giving people who have acted wrongly the power to influence not only what you believe but also who can influence your beliefs. This is bad in itself, but it also has harmful consequences. As we argue in Section 2.3, it can lead to problems when a person is accused of wrongdoing. In these cases, the word of the accused may be given more credibility than that of their accuser.

1.3 Moral Power

One way the immoral get moral power is through condonation of their wrongful behaviour. When you condone a piece of behaviour, you are communicating that while you do not think the behaviour is morally good, you are willing to accept or tolerate it (Hughes and Warmke 2017).[2] Suppose a friend mistreats you and you then condone their behaviour. You are not saying the friend's behaviour is good, but you are saying that you will not hold it against them. A problem with condoning wrongdoing is that it can sometimes *legitimate* that kind of behaviour – that is, it can make the wrongdoer believe that they can get away with acting this way. If you do not express to your friend that they have wronged you, they might think that their behaviour was acceptable. This is not only prudentially worrisome (they might not worry about being rude to you again in the future) but also morally problematic (they might come to think they can get away with rude behaviour in general). Expressing some moral disapproval is therefore necessary to avoid legitimating such behaviour.

One way honouring and admiring an immoral person condones their immoral behaviour is through *emotional prioritization*. If you choose to honour or admire an immoral person, you are choosing to pick them out as people others ought to admire rather than as people others ought to be indignant about. Given that these activities and emotions are all fitting – because a person can be both admirable and immoral – you are thereby communicating that this is the correct way to prioritize these attitudes and emotions. This can be communicated in different ways.

One way is through the meaning you intend your act to convey.[3] Suppose a man interrupts a woman and intends this interruption to express his sexist values. His act thereby has a sexist intentional meaning. If you intend an honour to condone a person's wrong, then the honour has this *intended meaning*.

When we condone immoral behaviour, it is often (perhaps even usually) not done so explicitly. A less explicit form of condonation stems from the *attitudinal meaning* of your acts of honouring or expressions of admiration for the immoral.[4] Acts express attitudes beyond those the person intends their act to express. Suppose a man interrupts a woman. The man may not intend this interruption to express sexist values. But it may express these values nevertheless, perhaps by conveying that he does not value the woman's contributions enough to let her finish her sentences. Similarly, when you honour and admire an immoral person you may communicate that you think that the person's immoral behaviour is acceptable or tolerable, even if you do not intend to convey this.

Actions also have a *public meaning*. This is the meaning that others can justifiably attribute to your acts given the context in which you perform them. The man who interrupts the woman may not have any sexist values, but he may interrupt her in a context in which it is reasonable or justifiable to understand his interruptions as revealing sexist attitudes or intentions – for example, in a business meeting in a company with a patriarchal working culture.

When you honour or admire the immoral this can have an adverse public meaning even if it does not in fact express any bad intentions or attitudes. Public meaning sometimes, but not always, stems from the structural and institutional context in which the action takes place. According to Sophie Hennekam and Dawn Bennett (2017), sexual harassment is a particular problem in the film industry due to its competitive nature, the culture within the industry, the industry's gendered power relations, and the importance of informal networks for career advancement. In such a context, choosing to honour and admire rather than condemn and blame a person who is also a rapist can reasonably be interpreted as condoning this behaviour. This sends the message that such behaviour can be ignored when the person performing it is sufficiently gifted. So, even if you neither intend to condone nor have attitudes that will express condonation, honouring and admiring an immoral person can still condone through being justifiably understood as condonation in the context in which they are honoured and admired.

While condonation often occurs through intended and attitudinal meaning, even when wrongful behaviour is condoned through public meaning alone, the immoral may gain the moral power to have their behaviour accepted or tolerated. Public meaning may then have the effect of making such behaviour seem justifiable or excusable. The fact that the immoral continue to be honoured and admired may make others justifiably believe that others think that the behaviour of the immoral is justifiable or excusable.

So far, we have looked at how public forms of honour and admiration can provide the target with moral power. However, admiring someone privately may do so as well. People often develop strong attachments to the public figures they admire (Thomson 2006). This can create a tension when the public figure acts immorally (Bhattacharjee et al. 2013). On the one hand, the admirer is attached to this figure and does not want to abandon their admiration. On the other hand, people are also generally attached to viewing themselves as morally decent, and admiring someone who has acted immorally may threaten this self-image. To resolve this tension, Bhattacharjee et al. (2013: 1169) suggest that admirers may revise their moral judgement so that they no longer view the act as morally wrong – a process known as moral rationalization.[5] In a series of studies, they found results consistent with this hypothesis.[6] So, even private admiration for someone who has acted immorally may give that person moral power, as it may lead the admirer to condone actions they would otherwise view as wrong.

1.4 Affective Power

One way the immoral may get affective power is through support. Andre Grahle (2019) proposes that in admiring people you *support* them in three ways. First, you give them *epistemic* support. You either give a person reason to believe that they are admirable or you reinforce their existing belief that they are admirable. Second, you give them *innervative* support. Sometimes you might still judge that a person is admirable but no longer admire them. When you see someone else admire the person, this can reinvigorate your admiration for them. Third, you give them *normative* support. This means that you give the admired person further reason to continue in their "admirable-making project" (Grahle 2019: 160). In Grahle's view, these reasons are petitionary – that is, the admirer expresses a desire that the admired person continue to possess their admirable properties. While Grahle focuses on reasons admirers give *the admired*, your admiration might also give reasons *to others* to admire those you admire. In other words, you can give epistemic, innervative, and normative support to others such that they come to admire those you admire.

While Grahle focuses on the positive aspects of support, it also has negative aspects. After all, the immoral can also be admirable. The problem with such support for immoral people stems from admiration's spreading feature. As we have discussed, when a person is admired for certain actions or traits, admirers often find themselves admiring, or at least looking positively upon, other parts of the person. For example, you admire a friend's patience with their child and then come to look more favourably upon their tardiness. Such spreading does not just occur for you, the admirer. It can also happen for the admired. When you admire a person for one thing, they may also come to see themselves as admirable for other things. For example, the friend you admire for being patient with their child might also come to see their tardiness as being admirable without your coming to admire their tardiness. Of course, if your admiration spreads from its initial ground, then this will serve to encourage the admired person's perception of the grounds of their admirability to spread too. And if other people's admiration spreads, then both your spreading and the admired person's spreading will receive further reinforcement.

The explanation for the spreading of admiration is that you start to connect other parts of the person, other sides of their character, and different ways they behave to their admirable properties. You might come to see these other parts as responsible for, or a necessary by-product of, what makes them admirable. In this way, you may look more favourably upon these other things or then also consider these other things to be admirable because of their relation to what you initially hold makes the person admirable. Consider again the friend who is always late because they are so patient with their child. They miss the start of meetings because they do not want to rush through interactions with their child. Because you admire them for being patient with their child, you come to think that their tardiness is a necessary by-product of such patience and because you desire them to keep being patient with their child, it is likely you will at least look more favourably upon their tardiness.

Another way to put this is that admiration spreads when you perceive other parts of the admired person as *connected to their admirable-making project*. Importantly, it does not matter what things are actually responsible or what things are really necessary by-products. Rather, it matters more what you take to be the responsible or necessary by-products. Because you think your friend has to be late all the time to continue being patient with their child, you see their tardiness in a more favourable light. It may well be that your friend can in fact continue being patient with their child and yet still make it on time to meet you. You can therefore give both the immoral person direct support for their immorality and give them indirect support by giving others reasons to admire them.

Affective power can be gained as a result of such support because it involves admiration spreading. When your admiration spreads, you may come to look more favourably upon these other parts of the person. Spreading is not necessarily bad. The fact the graduate student, from the example presented in Chapter 1, comes to dress like their supervisor might mean the student dresses better. However, you may find yourself feeling sympathy for those you admire and the struggles they have gone through. As such, you may give the admired person affective power over you. Even if your admiration does not spread, it might spread for others that you encourage to admire an immoral person. You may still, then, be giving the admired person affective power.

2 Harming Victims

The second general reason against honouring and admiring the immoral is that it leads to harms for the victims.[7] Beyond empowering perpetrators, there are at least three further ways victims may be harmed: disrespect, silencing, and complicity.

2.1 Disrespect

When the immoral are honoured and admired, a common complaint is that this disrespects their victims. For example, French actor Adèle Haenel said that awarding Roman Polanski a César award in 2020 was "spitting in the face of all victims. It means that raping isn't that bad" (Rosen 2020). This claim is often made with respect to statues of immoral figures, such as statues of confederate generals in the USA and colonialists in the UK and South Africa. For example, Johannes Schulz (2019) argues that statues degrade certain groups when they express a disrespectful ideology that is connected to ongoing or historical oppression of that group. And Ten-Herng Lai (2020) claims that statues commit *derogatory pedestaling* by implicitly ranking the victims of the honoured person as lesser than the honoured person. Honour and admiration for the immoral, then, may disrespect not only the victims of the honoured and admired immoral figure but also the victims of similar wrongdoers.

One possible understanding of what makes honouring and admiring an immoral person disrespectful is that such honouring and admiring involves an inappropriate emotional prioritization. It is disrespectful to honour and admire the immoral because it can be justifiably understood in certain contexts that you are saying that it is *more important* to honour and admire them than it is to blame and condemn them.

Another possible understanding of the disrespect claim is that it involves a failure to recognize the rights the victims have, the duties you have towards victims, or at least the moral reasons you have to modify your behaviour in light of the wrongs they have suffered. Schulz (2019) fleshes out the disrespect claim in terms of Stephen Darwall's notion of recognition respect. According to Darwall (1977: 40), to have recognition respect for something "is just to regard it as something to be reckoned with (in the appropriate way) and to act accordingly". When you are respectful in this way to a person, what you find acceptable to do is restricted such that you do not undermine the person's rights or affect the person's well-being without justification.

In order to avoid disrespecting victims of the immoral in this way, you must consider their desires and wishes. One way to do this is to ask them what they think about the perpetrator being honoured and admired. You show recognition respect for the fact that a person has been a victim of a crime if you check with them whether it is okay to invite the perpetrator to the same party as the victim. If you ask the victim and they are okay with the perpetrator coming to the party, then it may be permissible to invite them to the party without disrespecting the victim. Of course, this is not always going to be possible because some victims are dead and some victims might disagree with one another. And in some cases, victims might feel pressured into their choices. But even if you can, with some due diligence, avoid disrespecting the victims in Darwall's sense, you might still disrespect the victims of other similar crimes through inappropriate emotional prioritization, because you might still express a disrespectful prioritization of fitting emotions.

2.2 Silencing

Some wrongdoers might threaten their victims so that the victims do not speak out about the wrongs they have suffered. This can be done explicitly such that victims are given the expectation that they will not be believed if they do speak out. Whether or not they would actually be believed is another matter. What matters is what the victim expects to happen so that they do not think it is worth speaking out. In other words, the wrongdoer does not try to silence the victim directly but aims for the victim to silence themselves. This is what Kristie Dotson (2011) calls "testimonial smothering" – that is, a kind of self-silencing that people engage in when they expect that they will not be believed by a particular audience.

Such silencing not only occurs through the actions of the perpetrator; it may also happen as a side effect of honouring and admiring the immoral. Victims will (often justifiably) come to expect that people will not believe them *because* they were wronged by those that others honour and admire. Consider Louis CK's 2017 admission, which was subsequently published in *The New York Times*:

> I also took advantage of the fact that I was widely admired in my and their community, which disabled them from sharing their story and brought hardship to them when they tried because people who look up to me didn't want to hear it.

Louis CK is suggesting it was because he was admired that his accusers were not believed. This is in line with an earlier point we made: those you honour and admire often come to be seen to have greater credibility than they merit, which gives them a kind of epistemic power. There is harm to the victim purely in the fact that they may not be believed – what Miranda Fricker (2007) calls a testimonial injustice. While Fricker focuses on cases where a person's testimony is deemed to lack credibility because of their identity (e.g. being a child, being a woman, being a black person), we think honouring and admiring an immoral person can lead to those who challenge the immoral person's assertions to be seen as less credible *in comparison*.[8] Honouring and admiring elevates the immoral and in doing so contributes to inflating their credibility. By inflating their credibility, you in turn deflate the credibility of those who accuse them of wrongdoing – at least with respect to their testimony against the celebrity. This constitutes an indirect testimonial injustice for the victims.

But even if it is the case that victims would be believed if they spoke about how they were wronged, the fact that immoral people are typically honoured and admired without qualification may lead the victim to form the impression (correctly or incorrectly) that others see the immoral person as globally admirable. Such an impression generates the expectation that others will reject the victim's testimony because it conflicts with the image the victim believes others have of the immoral person. Given this expectation, it makes sense that victims do not speak out. They will find it safer to smother their own testimony – to silence themselves – because they fear that they will not be believed.

There is another reason why victims might silence themselves. In commenting upon a retrospective on Polanski's work that occurred in France in October 2017, Marlène Schiappa, the French Minister for Equality between Men and Women, highlighted that this honour was "contributing to the culture of rape by relativizing sexual aggression according to the celebrity of the perpetrator".[9] Schiappa's words crystallize a problem with condoning the acts of immoral artists: while people may say their acts are wrong, they do not respond to those acts *as wrongs*. As we have argued, this sends a bad message: people will be honoured even if they have done heinous things. This may also lead to a kind of hermeneutical injustice, which contributes to another kind of self-silencing.

The classic kind of hermeneutical injustice involves a person not having the conceptual resources to understand what wrong a particular harm constitutes. Miranda Fricker argues that prior to the coining of the term "sexual harassment" women struggled to understand the wrong they often suffered (Fricker 2007: 149–152). In this case, women lacked the conceptual resources to understand the injustice they faced. Katharine Jenkins (2017) argues that there is another kind of hermeneutical injustice. Sometimes people do not understand the injustice they face, even though they possess the relevant conceptual resources. For instance, many victims of rape do not consider themselves to be victims of rape (Burrowes 2013).[10]

To illuminate this type of hermeneutical injustice, Jenkins, following Haslanger (2012), notes that our "operative" concepts can sometimes differ from our "manifest" concepts. The latter is the formal definition of something, whereas the former is the practical use of that concept (which can differ from context to context). For example, being late to school might mean arriving after 8.50 (by decree of the headmaster). But if no teachers mark their pupils as late unless they arrive after 9.00, then *in practice* being late means arriving after 9.00. Here the operative concept of being late (arriving after 9.00) differs from the manifest concept of being late (arriving after 8.50). Importantly, what the concept is taken to mean depends on how the concept is used rather than what its formal definition is. The lateness case shows that it is not always harmful for an operative concept to stray from its manifest concept. However, there are also harmful cases. In particular, those victims of rape who do not consider themselves victims of rape seem to be working with an operative concept that harmfully strays from the manifest concept, leaving them unable to understand the way in which they have been wronged (Jenkins 2017: 196). Lacking awareness of the kind of injustice one faces makes it practically impossible to speak out about it. This adds further harm to the initial wrong (Jenkins 2017: 198).

Condoning sexual assault by honouring and admiring those who commit it contributes to maintaining these background hermeneutical injustices by perpetuating rape myths and cultural myths related to rape myths. For instance, it might make victims think they have not been raped. It might do so because they have been assaulted by a "great" person and support (and be supported by) what we will call *great person myths*. As we will discuss, one form of this myth involves the idea that great people cannot also be immoral. We may support this myth by not responding to wrongs *as wrongs*. Such responses might support the great person myth because victims have been assaulted by someone who does not seem like a perpetrator of rape, and so also support what we will call *perpetrator myths*. Victims might be unable to conceptualize their experience properly and so it is even harder for them to speak out about them. Even if they can conceptualize it properly, others may not. For example, others may not see some instances of sexual assault and sexual harassment involving great people or without the typical perpetrator as wrong. Such hermeneutical deficiencies may further contribute to the empowerment of perpetrators.

Such hermeneutical injustices do not just occur with sexual assault. They may also occur with respect to crimes related to anti-Semitism, sectarianism, racism, and the various forms of racial, national, and ethnic supremacism. If you honour and admire people who either endorse these ideologies or aspects of these ideologies, you may also condone (or appear to condone) those ideologies. This may contribute to distorting people's operative concepts of what is right and wrong as well as people's operative concepts of sexism, racism, and so on. Consequently, it may distort what exactly is wrong with sexism, racism, and so on. So even if people know that these ideologies and belief systems are mistaken and morally wrong, they may not take them to be wrong in practice. This may then lead people to struggle to take seriously other people's claims about sexism and racism. That honouring and admiring the immoral may contribute to this kind of hermeneutical injustice gives you some reason against honouring and admiring them. This meaning drift can also lead to another form of self-silencing on the behalf of victims.

Recall that Marlène Schiappa said that honouring Polanski was encouraging rape culture because there was something odd about telling people to speak up about sexual assault but then celebrating sexual predators. Because people's condonation of such wrongdoing encourages the idea that it is not in fact wrong, this also encourages a set of expectations. In particular, even when victims think they will be believed, they may come to expect (again often justifiably) that people will not care. This is a reasonable response to the fact that their assailant's behaviour has been condoned and supported, as well as to the fact they may have been disrespected through their assailant being honoured and admired. Once the idea that a great person's talents are more important than the crimes they have committed seems widely endorsed, the victim is likely to form the expectation that people will be indifferent to their suffering.

One particularly powerful way that this expectation can be supported is through the practice of *admiration bombing* – that is, reminding someone of a person's admirable qualities in an implicit or explicit effort to dismiss the accusations made against them. For example, in response to the controversy about Polanski being honoured with a retrospective, the French Minister for Culture dismissed the "ancient charges" against Polanski while reminding people that he is a "brilliant director" (Zaretsky 2017).

Another example of this occurred when New York University professor Avital Ronell was accused of sexually harassing, sexual assaulting, and stalking a student. A number of prominent academics – including the feminist scholar Judith Butler – signed an open letter in her defence. Of particular relevance is that the letter emphasized the signatories "enduring admiration" for Ronell. Moreover, they write,

> We testify to the grace, the keen wit, and the intellectual commitment of Professor Ronell and ask that she be accorded the dignity rightly deserved by someone of her international standing and reputation. If she were to be terminated or relieved of her duties, the injustice would be widely recognized and opposed.[11]

These things might well all be true of Ronell, while the accusations against her could nevertheless be true. Indeed, NYU determined that she had sexually harassed a student (Flaherty 2018).

And in 2004, Jacques Derrida also wrote a letter in defence of Dragan Kujundzic, a professor at University of California at Irvine (UCI) who had been accused of sexual harassment. Of particular relevance, Derrida wrote that:

> I know Dragan better and longer than anyone at Irvine. For more than twenty years, I have followed and admired his work, his intelligence, his rigor, and his integrity, his strict sense of ethical, intellectual, and academic responsibility. (In particular, I know him to be absolutely incapable of using or abusing his power with students, abuse being implied, in the strict sense, by the concept of "sexual harassment").[12]

Derrida bombards us with details about the accused's admirable qualities as a defence against accusations of sexual harassment. Again, one can be both admirable *and* immoral, so highlighting these qualities is completely irrelevant. It is not surprising that so many people smother their own testimony when this kind of practice is prevalent.

2.3 Complicity

Another way you can harm victims is through honour and admiration making you complicit in the wrongs of those you honour and admire. Suppose your friend commits a crime and you let them plan the crime at your house. You do not actually commit the crime, but given your assistance, you are complicit in the crime because you contributed to the crime coming about. You might think that when you honour or admire an immoral person that you cannot be complicit because you have not helped them commit the relevant crimes. For example, you have not arranged for an artist to sexually harass a fan. But, with respect to athletes, artists, and intellectuals, we do often give them money. We pay for their films, music, books, and to see them in person. We give them the means to have the power and opportunity to engage in particular types of immorality. In this way, we are complicit in their immorality.

Of course, this is not a reason against honouring and admiring the immoral in general. Rather, it is a reason against giving them your money. While this arguably counts as a form of honouring as money is scarce resource, it is adaptable into a reason against honouring and admiring them in general. Notice that often what gives the immoral the power and opportunity to act wrongly is their *fame*. One thing that can influence their fame is their financial power. Another factor is how honoured and admired the person is (which, as discussed in Section 1, may affect how much financial power they have). The more honoured and admired a person is the more famous they typically are. Not only do honours and admiration often make a person more famous, but they also often contribute towards a person having various sorts of power identified in Section 1. It is in part because they have various kinds of power that people can continue to act immorally and often get away with it. By honouring and admiring an immoral person, you contribute to their fame and power, which gives them opportunities to act immorally. In this way, we are complicit in their immorality.

You might object that the individual contributions towards a person's power and fame that you make by honouring and admiring them are so small that your contributions do not really make a difference and so you are not really complicit. This objection allows that significant instances of public honouring and admiration may make a difference. So, giving an Oscar to a predatory filmmaker, a retrospective to a sexist painter, and a lifetime achievement award to an anti-Semitic intellectual are potentially ways to be complicit in another's immorality. Moreover, due to their epistemic power, a famous person who openly admires a genocidal tyrant might also be complicit in the tyrant's immorality. However, individuals with everyday social status just cannot have the same kind of effect. Or so the objection goes.

It is true that institutions, such as The Academy, and other major honourers and admirers seem like clear cases of those who should be concerned about being complicit in the wrongs of the immoral. However, even if individuals may have less to worry about here because they are likely to be less complicit than institutions, this does not mean they have no reason to worry. Individuals may still have to be concerned about honouring and admiring the immoral based on what *other people* are doing. To compare, leaving your lights on or having baths every day might be fine if you are the only person doing it. However, the permissibility of doing so depends on what other people are doing. If everyone is using excessive water or electricity, then it will lead to a harmful outcome that should be avoided. Because we live in an interconnected world, what we have moral reason to do or not do sometimes depends on what other people are doing. While the debate about collective action problems remains and we make no attempt to solve it, we think it is reasonable for you to take into consideration that you might be complicit with the wrongs of the immoral to some extent if you honour and admire them.[13]

3 Perpetuating Wrongdoing

The third general reason against honouring and admiring the immoral is that it perpetuates wrongdoing. There are at least two ways it can do so: emulation and ideology.

3.1 Emulation

When you honour or admire a person, this also functions to identify them as an exemplar – that is, as someone to be emulated. In Polanski's case, his honour of being appointed as president of the César awards identifies him as an exemplar. Because this is an honour for *aesthetic* achievement it is reasonable to think that Polanski is only being identified as an aesthetic exemplar. Given this, it might seem that such an honour is unproblematic because it is only passing judgement on his aesthetic abilities and not his moral behaviour. Likewise, if a person expresses admiration for Hans Asperger in an article detailing the reasons why they think he was a great doctor and medical scientist, the person might simply take themselves to be identifying him as an intellectual exemplar. Again, this might seem unproblematic because they may only take themselves to be passing judgement on Asperger's epistemic abilities and achievements and not his moral behaviour. Perhaps the most vivid form of exemplar identification involves those immoral figures who are depicted in statues. Such people are literally put on a pedestal, and it is hard to deny that when this happens they are being identified as exemplars. Again, though, you might think the statue just honours their achievements and not their immorality.

However, given admiration's spreading tendency, when you admire one feature of a person, this sometimes leads you admiring (or looking more favourably upon) other features of the person as well. For example, a teenager's admiration for their favourite footballer's sporting abilities may lead them to admire their political views. Once admiration spreads to these features this may then lead to a desire to emulate these aspects of the person as well. We may identify these as part of the person's admirable-making project and then try to emulate those aspects. Given that we pick the immoral out as people we ought to admire when we honour or admire them, we have reason to worry about honouring and admiring them, as this may lead people to emulate the immoral in other ways.

We are not suggesting that anyone is going to commit sexual assault as a direct result of admiring Polanski's artistic talent. Or that anyone is going to contribute to mass murder as a direct result of admiring Asperger's intellectual abilities. But emulating exemplars need not involve straightforward imitation. As Kristján Kristjánsson (2006: 41) argues, the proper role of exemplars is to "help you arrive at an articulate conception of what you value and want to strive towards". Emulation should therefore be seen as a process by which one attempts to achieve these values. Even if it does not lead anyone to imitate them, identifying an immoral person as an exemplar can be bad because it encourages people to pursue or uphold problematic ideals. In the case of Polanski, those ideals may include great person myths, which may justify or excuse wrongdoing if it is done in the service of artistic greatness. The fact that honouring and admiring the immoral can lead to such emulation gives us another moral reason not to honour and admire the immoral.

3.2 Ideology

It is often said that honouring and admiring the immoral perpetuates morally reprehensible *ideologies* (e.g. Burch-Brown 2017; Schulz 2019). For example, honouring Polanski has been claimed to perpetuate rape culture (e.g. Schiappa's comments cited in Zaretsky 2017), and honouring Confederate generals with statues in the USA has been claimed to perpetuate white supremacism (e.g. Lopez 2017; Schulz 2019; Rossi 2020).

According to Sally Haslanger, "ideology functions to stabilize or perpetuate unjust power and domination, and does so through some form of masking or illusion" (2017a: 150). In other words, ideologies are always bad because they mislead us about the nature of reality and value. Following Stuart Hall (1996), Joanna Burch-Brown (2017: 65, fn.16) points out that one need not conceive of an ideology in normatively negative terms as Haslanger does – that is, an ideology need not be bad. On this normatively neutral understanding, ideology is the set of tools and resources that we use to understand social reality and to give us guidance on how to act. According to Haslanger (2017b), these tools and resources include aspects of our psychologies that lead to beliefs and judgements, such as schemas, which are ways we process and categorize people, objects, and events. These tools and resources also include social meanings, symbols, and practices. Central to this conception of ideology is the idea that there are looping effects between these internal and external aspects of ideology. We have the schemas we have in part because of the social meanings, symbols, and practices we have. And we have the latter in part because of the schemas we have. It is because of this looping effect that a particular resource, tool, or practice can seem to be correct, reliable, or a "given". In particular, your conception of your social reality might seem obvious to you, but it may also be the result of an implicit ideology. Whether you can avoid ideology in some form or whether ideologies are always bad is an open question. Even so, we think it is clear that ideology is something we should at least be wary of contributing to, as there are clear cases of ideologies that perpetuate wrongdoing. How do honouring and admiring practices support harmful ideologies? Burch-Brown (2017) argues that statues of people – particularly those involved in grave injustices such as the transatlantic slave trade – can support harmful ideologies (such as racism and white supremacism)[14] by (i) honouring those who endorsed such ideologies (or aspects of such ideologies), (ii) expressing a particular identity, and (iii) sending a signal about who has power and authority in the community. Statues can do so in part because of their typical placement. For example, they are often placed in prominent places where they draw lots of attention. Because a decision has been made to place this statue in such an attention-focused space, it can communicate quite a strong message about the values and ideals of the community.

Relatedly, statues can support harmful ideologies through what Ten-Herng Lai (2020) calls *derogatory pedestaling*. According to Lai, by declaring an immoral person as honourable through creating (and maintaining) a statue of them, the statue indirectly ranks the honoured person's victims as inferior. This is because the honour only makes sense against a background belief that those oppressed by the target of the honour are inferior and of lesser moral worth than other people. Honouring a slave trader, for example, only makes sense if we do not value those whose lives were ruined by the slave trade. Moreover, when these honours are given by a national or local government, they may claim to speak in the name of the state's citizens or a local region's population. These should be understood as instances of political speech that are capable of functioning as a form of expressive harm. By communicating that a group of people are inferior this reinforces the idea that this group of people really are inferior. So, a statue can in effect be an external resource in a harmful ideology. It is supported by particular internal tools and resources (such as schema) and in turn helps to support those internal tools and resources.

Support for harmful ideologies need not just occur through statues. You might support these ideologies, to some extent, whenever you honour and admire an immoral person. For example, when you honour and admire someone, you pick them out as an exemplar, as someone who ought to be admired, and, in doing so, you may suggest that they are worthy of being emulated. As we said earlier, such emulation need not be literal. For example, you might not try to sail ships from Africa to the Americas with slaves. But you might try to emulate the values of the person you honour and admire or the person you see others honouring and admiring. By honouring and admiring someone you are often putting them on a pedestal, and in doing so you may appear to suggest that these are at least tolerable values. In addition, you may appear to be disrespecting the victims of the person as well as the victims of similar crimes. In at least these ways, honouring and admiring the immoral supports harmful ideologies. Indeed, it may well result from such ideologies too; as we discussed, that there is a looping effect between wrongs and ideologies is part of what makes ideologies hard to challenge and dislodge.

We will now identify two schemas of harmful ideologies that we think are both promoted by honouring and admiring the immoral and support, directly or indirectly, various injustices. Note three things. First, we do not think these schemas should be character- ized as essential features of these ideologies – for example, racism and supremacism could exist without them. Even so, we think they can at least indirectly support these and other harmful ideologies. Second, we think these schemas are bad in and of themselves. So even if they did not support harmful ideologies, the fact we might promote these still gives reasons against honouring and admiring the immoral. Third, we do not think honouring and admiring the immoral is the only source of these schemas. Indeed, these schemas may also at least partially explain why we honour and admire the immoral or why we honour and admire them in the ways we of- ten do. Again, this is to be expected given the looping effects that Haslanger outlines. The two schemas we identify are two related cultural myths that we mentioned earlier.

Great Person Myths. One kind of great person myth is related to what Manne (2017: 180) calls the "honorable Brutus" problem. The idea is that we are presented with a great person and then we are presented with the wrongdoing they have committed. Because we take the person to be great, this gives us a basis for denying that they did anything wrong.[15] This myth is another source of epistemic power. Another kind of great person myth is that doing something great enough either justifies or renders tolerable wrongs a person might have committed. This myth is another source of moral power.

Both kinds of myth are present in the honouring and admiring of certain immoral political figures. For example, Christopher Columbus is honoured yearly on Columbus Day. He is honoured for discovering the Americas for Europeans, but he is thought to have brutalized and oppressed many of the indigenous peoples that he came across. Despite his animosity towards black South Africans, his attitude towards women, and his endorsement of the caste system, Mahatma Gandhi is still revered for his role in securing India's independence through peaceful protests (Sen 2015). The honouring and admiring of such political figures encourages both myths because the focus is usually exclusively on the great things that they did.[16] And when their wrongdoing is brought up, many people either do not accept that they did anything wrong, that they must have been justified in what they did, or that they think we should just accept that they did these things because it was a necessary by-product of their greatness. The end result is that we may end up understanding other admirable people according to such schemas (greatness is incompatible with badness; greatness justifies badness; greatness makes badness tolerable) in part because our honouring and admiring of such people expresses and supports such myths.

Perpetrator Myths. Audrey Yap (2017) argues that in cases of sexual assault that we often rely on certain myths about what perpetrators of sexual assault are like. She argues that because our "standard stories" (i.e., schemas about sexual assault) involve perpetrators who are either mentally ill or thoroughly vicious and irredeemable, we have trouble acknowledging that ordinary people can commit sexual assault. She proposes that we expand our stories or paradigms about sexual assault to include those that involve sexual assault committed by otherwise ordinary people who are neither mentally ill nor evil and who are capable of maintaining normal relationships with friends and family. Honouring and admiring the immoral may feed the myth that perpetrators (of sexual assault and other wrongs) are like this by emphasizing the problematic standard stories that Yap identifies. (Indeed, this is likely an offshoot of the great person myths we discussed above.) Perhaps because admiration has a tendency to spread, we may come to see those who are honoured and admired as wholly admirable and so unable to be guilty of terrible crimes. Our current honour and admiration practices may implicitly encourage the myth that perpetrators must be either be mentally ill or thoroughly evil by focusing attention on an admirable person's positive qualities and actions and overlooking their negative qualities and actions.

4 Responding to These Reasons

The general reasons we have identified are present in some but not all cases. For example, sometimes honouring and admiring the immoral will empower them, but sometimes not. Even when those reasons are present in a particular case, they can vary in strength. For example, sometimes honouring and admiring the immoral will harm the victims but not very much. In this section, we will go through certain questions you should ask yourself when trying to figure out whether you should, all-things-considered, honour and admire the immoral.

First, what is the wrong? Noticeably, many of the points we made concern wrongs to victims and wrongs relating existing (structural, systemic) injustices. So, certain wrongs will avoid (or largely avoid) the reasons against honouring and admiring the immoral. For example, the fact that Winona Ryder is a convicted shoplifter does not seem to give you much reason not to honour and admire her for her acting. In particular, it is not a very significant wrong, and it does not seem to perpetuate a bad ideology. You must, then, establish what the wrong is and whether and to what extent it exacerbates the moral dangers we have identified. Take Roman Polanski's sexual assault on Samantha Geimer. This is a significant crime, so you should be concerned about the moral dangers of honouring and admiring Polanski.

Second, who are you? That is, are you an individual or an institution? We have largely spoken about reasons against honouring and admiring the immoral regardless of who the honourer or admirer is. Yet who the honourer or admirer is does seem to make a difference to the strength of the moral reasons. There is a stronger reason for an institution such as *The Academy*, which gives out The Oscars, not to honour and admire Polanski than there is for an individual. Then again, it also depends on who the individual is. A celebrity with a lot of influence has a stronger reason against honouring and admiring than a mere individual, because a celebrity typically has more influence and epistemic power than a mere individual (Archer et al. 2020). The influence of the institution also makes a difference. A local film club has a weaker reason not to give Polanski a retrospective than a national film body. You must, then, think about who you are and in what capacity you will be honouring and admiring a person. If your contribution is particularly small, then it is acceptable for you to continue honouring or admiring a particular immoral person. But if your contribution is large enough, then perhaps you should not honour or admire a particular immoral person.

Third, what are other people doing? While you might act as an individual, your actions do not occur in a vacuum. Even small acts can be unintentionally part of a larger group effort. As we discussed earlier, this is a kind of collective action problem that is similar in structure to the problem of contributing to climate change. Your individual contribution does not seem to make a difference and yet every person's contribution taken as a whole does make a difference. The important point for us is that even if you are not to blame or have no obligation not to make contributions to climate change, you can still have moral reasons not to contribute. Likewise, if your small act of honouring and admiring an immoral person will contribute to one of the moral dangers, then you may have reason, albeit a weak one, not to honour and admire.

Fourth, how are you going to honour and admire? It matters what form your honour and admiration takes. Individuals may well privately honour and admire an immoral person. Do these moral reasons speak against that? Yes, but in many cases the reason will not be very strong. For example, it still disrespects Polanski's victim if you privately honour him with a poster in your bedroom. But the strength of the reasons against honouring him with a poster seem quite weak – especially, as we discuss in the next chapter, if you have some deep personal connection with Polanski's work. If you represent an institution that is planning to give a lifetime achievement award to an immoral person, then the reasons against are going to be much stronger because this will likely be understood as a global endorsement of the awardee. If you are going to give a more specific award, the reasons will be weaker, because it is less likely to be understood as global endorsement of the person. The strength of the reasons will also differ depending how much influence the institution has. In some cases, though, as we discuss in the next chapter, the criteria for the honour will be firm so you will be obliged to honour an immoral person.

Fifth, what is the context of your honouring and admiring? Noticeably, the reasons against grounded in points about public meaning – such as those about empowering the perpetrator – rely significantly on the context in which one honours and admires. It is worth making clear that these reasons are much stronger if one's honour and admiration condones the immoral person's behaviour through intentional or attitudinal meaning rather than through public meaning. One reason we make our points in terms of public meaning is that this shows that even if you do not have bad intentions or attitudes (as some people may claim in defence of why *they* should be fine to honour and admire the immoral) you can still have moral reason against honouring and admiring the immoral. If we focus just on public meaning, this allows that there are possible and actual contexts in which honouring and admiring the immoral will not have an adverse public meaning. So, reasons made in terms of public meaning are not decisive. We think, though, that if our acts of honouring and expressions of admiration have a bad intentional or attitudinal meaning, then our reasons based on these meanings are much stronger. Even so, it is not clear that these reasons are decisive independent of a particular context.

Some might worry that there is no problem with our actions having an adverse public meaning. They might think that we should not be blamed if others read things into our actions and emotions that are not expressive of our own intentions or attitudes. The objection is that blame lies with others and not with us. Even though others may be blameworthy for reading things into actions and emotions that are not expressive of the agent's intentions or attitudes, we see no reason why this precludes people from having a responsibility to think about what others might read into their actions. If a comedian thinks their ironic racist joke, which they intend to lampoon racists, will be used as a slogan by neo-Nazis to galvanize a popular movement, then this could give them reason not to tell it. It is true that the context-sensitive nature of public meaning can make it difficult to determine. But even if it is difficult to determine, this does not mean we always lack such a reason against honouring and admiring. Consider clear cases, such as the giving of awards. Given the way that awards are typically given, with all the fanfare and celebration of the awardee, they can clearly be perceived as condoning the immoral behaviour of the awardee. It is plausible, then, that such honourers have a responsibility to consider how others will interpret the giving of an award to an immoral person. Again, though, the reason is not decisive.

Moreover, we can perhaps still have moral reasons against honouring and admiring the immoral even when the bad meaning that some people will take from a person's being honoured and admired is not justified. In applying several of our points to debates about statues of immoral people, Benjamin Rossi (2020), drawing on Dan Demetriou and Ajume Wingo (2018), identifies another form of public meaning – namely, the meaning that others will take whether or not it is justified. For example, some might take a man's interruption of a woman to be sexist regardless of whether it is justified to understand the man's action this way or not. Rossi argues for the importance of such meaning in the context of statues of immoral or controversial political figures. Sometimes we should take down a statue even when the adverse meaning some people find in it is not justified. Arguably, though, moral reasons against honouring and admiring are much weaker in cases where people will mistakenly infer a bad meaning.

Finally, is the proposed target of honour and admiration alive? The reasons against honouring and admiring a wrongdoer may lose much of their force after their death. For instance, we have little reason to worry about effects of empowering a person who is no longer alive to use that power. However, the death of an admired person does not fully eliminate these worries. By honouring and admiring someone after their death we may be empowering their supporters, which may in turn harm their victims. For example, continuing to honour and admire Michael Jackson after his death may aid those who were attempting to silence the voices of those making sexual assault allegations against him. In addition, this honour and admiration could serve to empower those committing similar wrongs by perpetuating a negative ideology that serves to underplay the significance of their wrongdoing. So while death may influence these reasons, it would be wrong to conclude that the reasons against honouring and admiring an immoral person do not apply if that person is dead.

In answering all these questions (and perhaps others), you might find that you have decisive reason to abandon honour and admiration for a particular immoral person who is a fitting target of admiration. We think that in some cases there are decisive reasons against honouring and admiring. We think statues of immoral political leaders are a clear case. Even though some (though far from all) of those depicted in statues are admirable in some way, we often should not depict them in statues. In Chapter 5, we argue that this is because statues typically encourage or manifest the vice of globalism. But we do not think there is justification for abandoning honour and admiration in all cases. The fact that the reasons against honouring and admiring the immoral that we have identified in this chapter are not decisive in all cases supports this conclusion. In the next chapter, we consider general reasons against abandoning admiration – namely, *reasons to* honour and admire the immoral. While these reasons do not establish that we should never abandon admiration, they do help to further highlight that we cannot abandon admiration in all cases. In other words, sometimes we should, all-things-considered, honour and admire the immoral.

Notes

1 The concept of epistemic power comes from Geuskens (2018).
2 For more on condonation and how it differs from forgiveness, see, for example, Pettigrove (2004).
3 Intended meaning is similar to what Grice (1957) calls non-natural meaning and has become known as *speaker meaning*. Since we take intended meaning to go beyond speech acts, we prefer our terminology.
4 Our use of "attitudinal meaning" is similar to McKenna's (2012) "agent meaning". Rossi (2020: 51) worries that attitudinal meaning might be misunderstood because intentions are a kind of attitude. He therefore recommends calling this "implicit meaning". As we make clear what we take attitudinal meaning to cover, we hope that readers will not misunderstand our terminology.
5 Relatedly, a study by Paharia and Deshpandé (2009) found that the more people desire to own a product the more likely they are to excuse the use of sweatshop labour in its production.
6 Though Bhattacharjee et al.'s main interest in these studies is in moral decoupling, where people separate judgements of performance from judgements of morality. We will discuss this in Chapter 5.
7 For another perspective on this point, see Elicker (forthcoming).
8 See Medina (2011) for an account of a general link between credibility excess and credibility deficit. We identify a more specific link that is compatible with Medina's account.
9 Quote taken from Zaretsky (2017).
10 According to Burt (1980: 217), rape myths are "prejudicial, stereotyped, or false beliefs about rape, rape victims, and rapists". Lonsway and Fitzgerald (1994: 135) propose refining this definition such that rape myths "are attitudes and beliefs that are generally false but are widely and persistently held, and that serve to deny and justify male sexual aggression against women". While we agree that rape myths most often serve to deny and justify male sexual aggression against women, this definition may perpetuate two other rape myths – namely that men cannot be victims of rape and that women cannot rape. As Curry (2017) points out, these myths help to cover up the sexual victimization of black men in the United States. So, we instead suggest that rape myths are attitudes and beliefs that are generally false but are widely and persistently held that serve to deny and justify sexual aggression.
11 See Leiter (2018).
12 For the full letter, see http://www.jacques-derrida.org/Cicerone.html
13 For more on complicity and collective responsibility, see Kutz (2000) and McPherson (2015).
14 Haslanger (2017b: 16–17) argues that racism is not an ideology but an ideological formation. This is because on her view ideology consists of cultural techne (tools), whereas racism "is constituted by an interconnected web of unjust social practices that unjustly disadvantage certain groups, e.g., residential segregation, police brutality, biased hiring and wage inequity, educational disadvantage, etc.". While racism is supported by and itself supports *racist* techne, she holds these should

be distinguished. We elide this distinction in what follows as nothing of substance hangs on making it.

15 Yap (2017: 16) makes the same kind of point. Both Yap and Manne are more concerned with the effect this myth has on the testimony of those who accuse a great person of wronging them.

16 See Berninger (forthcoming) for a fictionalist account of commemoration that provides a justification for overlooking the commemorated person's immorality.

4 Against Abandoning Admiration

So far, we have argued that it is possible for the immoral to be admirable but that there can also be important moral reasons that count against actually honouring and admiring them. Does this mean that we should abandon all honour and admiration of the immoral? No, because the general reasons we identified are not decisive in all cases. There are also important reasons that count against abandoning honour and admiration in these cases – namely, reasons to honour and admire the immoral. These reasons might also be thought to support a popular claim that it would be wrong to abandon our admiration of people on the basis of their immoral behaviour. While our focus is on the force of these reasons, our discussion also reveals that this claim is mistaken because all the reasons we identify are not in general decisive.

We focus on four reasons. First, that the admirable deserve honour and admiration and so it would be wrong to deny them this. Second, that allowing morality to fully dictate the people we admire would be a form of overly judgemental moralism. Third, that in refusing to admire or honour the immoral we would be shutting ourselves off from distinctive contributions and insights into the human condition. Finally, that because our admiration for people can play an important role in our sense of identity, morality should not require us to abandon admiration that has this kind of personal value. We will argue that each of these arguments identifies an important consideration that should inform the ethics of honouring and admiring. They identify reasons that you must also consider when trying figure out whether you should honour and admire an immoral person. As we show that these reasons are not decisive in all cases, we also show that the reasons do not support doing nothing as a policy.

DOI: 10.4324/9780367810153-4

1 Fittingness, Desert, and Entitlement

In 2011, Roman Polanski travelled to Switzerland to collect a lifetime achievement award from the Zurich Film Festival. The honour was originally awarded in 2009, but the Swiss police had arrested the director on a warrant relating to the rape of 13-year-old Samantha Geimer in 1977. The decision to give this honour to Polanski was unsurprisingly controversial given his crime. However, while there were many who criticized the decision to honour Polanski in this way, there were also those who defended the decision. Some of these defenders sought to downplay the significance of the crime. Others accepted the severity of Polanski's crime but argued that Polanski nevertheless deserved the award. For example, in an opinion piece in *The Guardian*, Hannah Slapper (2011) argued that Polanski should be given the award despite the "repulsive" nature of his crime. Slapper defended this view in the following way:

> In regards to this award, his personal history is entirely irrelevant. [...] By rewarding these people for the things they have created, they are not forgiving them their crimes. *Polanski deserves this recognition.* He's contributed greatly to the cause of film, and that is all that matters.
>
> (Slapper 2011; emphasis added)

Slapper's point is that Polanski deserves this honour and that not only does this give us reason to award it to him, nothing else counts against him receiving this honour.

Similar points are often made in discussions about whether to honour and admire the immoral, whether they be artists, intellectuals, or politicians. For example, Andrew Roberts, who wrote a biography of Winston Churchill, claimed that criticisms of Churchill are "unimportant, all of them, compared to the centrality of the point of Winston Churchill, which is that he saved [Britain] from being invaded by the Nazis" (Adam 2015). Again, the point seems to be that whatever else Churchill may have done, he deserves to be honoured for this achievement. The underlying thought here is that all those who achieve great things deserve to be honoured and admired. Call this claim the *deservingness of admiration.*

Claiming that someone *deserves* admiration is a stronger claim than the claim that admiration is *fitting.* The fittingness claim is a claim about the accuracy of the evaluation involved in admiration.

If someone is a fitting target of admiration, then it is accurate to view that person as being excellent in some way and meriting positive evaluation and wonder. This excellence may be due to their artistic talents, their intellectual achievements, their service to their nation, or something else entirely. When we say that admiration is fitting for someone, we are saying that those who feel admiration for that person are representing the world accurately. Saying that someone *deserves* admiration goes beyond this to make a moral claim. From the moral point of view, people ought to get what they deserve.[1] So by making the desert claim we are saying that not only would admiration for this person be a response that accurately represents the world but also that, morally, this person ought to be admired.[2]

This claim about the deservingness of admiration has two parts. There is a claim about the basis of desert (achieving excellent things), and there is a claim about the treatment that is deserved (honour and admiration). Both parts of this claim should be accepted. There are at least two ways to support the claim about the basis of desert.[3] First, one might argue that the basis for being awarded a prize, a paradigmatic form of honouring, is the possession of a skill (Feinberg 1970: 226). But the mere possession of a skill is unlikely to be a sufficient basis for deserving an award. The skill must also be manifested in some achievement that will serve as the basis of the award. An award for best director, for example, awards the director's skill as it is manifested in a particular film. Achieving great things as a result of one's skills and talents is then a plausible basis for deserving honour and admiration.

Second, one might appeal to an institutional desert basis. According to institutional views of desert (e.g. Arnold 1987; Cummiskey 1987), the bases on which people are deserving of certain forms of treatment are dependent on the goals of the institution providing the form of treatment. If the goal of a film award ceremony is to reward the best filmmakers of the past year, then making the best contribution to cinema is the basis for deserving an award. Similarly, if the goal of statues commemorating political figures is to acknowledge those who have contributed to the good of the nation, then having achieved great things for one's country is the basis for deserving a statue in one's honour.[4]

Similarly, a plausible case can be made to support the claim about deserved treatment. There is good reason to think that the various ways in which people can deserve to be treated by others tend to be affective in nature (Feinberg 1970: 225). People can deserve to be praised or blamed, admired or held in contempt, rewarded or punished, celebrated or denigrated. These are all affective responses, and, according to Feinberg (1970: 225), if we lacked any affective responses such as these, "then there would be no use for the concept of desert". Even if we do not accept this strong claim, it is undeniable that the kinds of treatment that people can deserve are *often* affective in nature. If people can deserve some kind of affective treatment on the basis of achieving great things, then admiration and honour are the most plausible candidates, as these are the affective responses we typically take to be deserved by those who have achieved great things.

The deservingness of admiration by itself, though, does not tell us anything about what other people should do in relation to this deservingness. To support this kind conclusion, we need to add the claim that the fact people deserve honour and admiration gives others moral reason to honour and admire them. Put in the strongest terms, this deservingness is claimed by some to generate a moral requirement to admire. Michael Zimmerman puts the point in this way:

> Even if there is no (direct) moral requirement to *display* any of the nonmoral virtues, there is nonetheless, as has been acknowledged, a requirement to *admire* them when they are displayed. What sort of a requirement is this? Surely the answer is: *moral.* It is *morally* fitting that one admire all virtues, *whether or not* the virtues themselves are moral. Likewise, it is *morally* fitting that one reprehend all vices, *whether* or *not* the vices themselves are moral.
>
> (1999: 11; original emphasis)

Zimmerman's claim is that we have a moral requirement to admire those who display non-moral virtue, such as artistic talent or intellectual greatness. We will call this claim the *duty to give people what they deserve.*

If we put together the *deservingness of admiration* and the *duty to give people what they deserve*, then we can make a simple argument for the conclusion that we ought to honour and admire the immoral despite their immorality.

Premise 1: All those who achieve great things deserve honour and admiration. (Deservingness of Admiration)[5]
Premise 2: People have a duty to ensure that others get the things they deserve. (Duty to give people what they deserve)
Conclusion: People have a duty to ensure that those who achieve great things receive honour and admiration.

Despite there being something to this argument, it should not be accepted in its current form. The reason for this is that the idea that there is a duty to give people what they deserve should only be accepted if it is significantly weakened. As it stands this claim holds that people have a *duty* to ensure others get what they deserve. This suggests that desert claims will always win out against other moral considerations. This view is implausible for at least three reasons.

First, there can be a conflict between different desert claims. For example, in a race the person who crosses the finishing line in first place deserves to receive the gold medal. However, it may be the case that they did not deserve to win the race. Perhaps the fastest runner suffered some bad luck and twisted their ankle 10 meters from the finishing line. According to Feinberg (1970: 227), in this kind of case, "the person who deserves the prize is not the person who deserves to win it". The claim that people always ought to get what they deserve, regardless of the other moral considerations in play, generates very odd results in this case. The winner of the race ought, all things considered, to receive the gold medal because they won the race and so deserves the gold medal. However, there is another runner who deserved to win the race and, if they had got what they deserved, would then deserve to receive the gold medal. So giving both runners what they deserve in this case would mean giving the gold medal to both of them. This is an absurd result and suggests that people do not always have a duty to ensure others get what they deserve.

Second, desert claims can also conflict with *entitlement* claims and where they do the entitlement claim should generally take priority. As Feinberg (1970: 231) points out, someone may deserve a reward but not be entitled to one. In other words, it does not automatically follow from the fact that someone deserves to be treated in some way that they have a *right* to be treated in that way. Conversely, someone may be entitled to a reward they do not deserve. Feldman and Skow (2019) give the following example that highlights both points well. Suppose a wealthy grandfather has two grandchildren, one who is virtuous and devoted and the other who is vicious and disloyal. It is reasonable to think that the virtuous grandchild deserves at least as much of the inheritance as the vicious grandchild. However, if the grandfather leaves all his fortune to the vicious grandchild then they are entitled to all of it, and the virtuous grandchild is entitled to none of it. In this case, if both grandchildren were to receive what they deserve, then the virtuous grandchild would receive more than is stipulated in the will and the vicious grandchild would receive less. However, the fact that this is what would be deserved does not settle the issue of what ought to happen. We might think that even if the virtuous grandchild does deserve some of the inheritance, the fact that they are not entitled to it means that all things considered they ought not to receive any of it.

Finally, desert claims can also be in conflict with the action that would bring about the best consequences. To return to the previous example, suppose that the virtuous grandchild is an incredibly talented research scientist doing important work in developing medicines for currently untreatable disease. Moreover, if they receive the share of the inheritance that they deserve they will become lazy and give up their job as a researcher, setting back the development of these medicines and leading to thousands of lives being lost as a result. It is at least an open question whether the grandchild ought, all things considered, to receive the inheritance in this case. Again though, if we accept the strong interpretation of the deservingness claim then there should be no open question here. If the grandchild deserves the inheritance then, according to the duty to give others what they deserve, others have a duty to ensure the grandchild receives it.

Given these problems with the duty to give others what they deserve, we should accept a weaker version of this claim according to which people have *some moral reason to give others what they deserve.*[6] This means that the claim that Polanski deserves a particular form of recognition does not provide a decisive reason to think that he ought to receive it. Rather, it means that he ought to receive it unless there are good reasons that count against doing so. If such reasons exist, then we will have to do the difficult work of deciding which of these reasons win out in this particular case. It is also worth noting that this reason to give people what they deserve will not apply to everyone. There is, after all, no reason to think that those with interest in cinema have any reason to ensure that Polanski receives any form of honour or admiration. The revised conclusion, then, should read as follows:

> Revised Conclusion: *Some* people have *some* moral reason to ensure that those who achieve great things receive honour and admiration.

In the case of honour and admiration, the reasons that count in favour of ensuring people get what they deserve will have to be considered alongside the three broad types of reason that may count against honouring and admiring the immoral. For any particular case of admiring the immoral, when one or more of these reasons exists, we will have to engage in the difficult business of deciding which set of reasons is decisive. In order to make this judgement, we should consider several broad considerations that may influence the strength of the desert claim. First, desert claims may also be entitlement claims. This is not always the case, but where it is the case, the reasons in favour of honouring and admiring will be stronger. In the case of honours, desert claims governed by formal criteria are especially likely to ground entitlement claims. The winner of a 100-metre race, for example, is entitled to the gold medal, as this award is governed by strict criteria. For other forms of honour, the criteria are less clear and so it will also be less clear whether someone is entitled to that honour. We can therefore say that when an honour is governed by strict formal criteria, it is more likely to be the case that the target of the honour not only deserves this honour but is also entitled to it.

But while someone can be entitled to an honour, Feinberg argues that one cannot be entitled to the admiration of others, even though one can deserve it:

> Praise and blame, admiration and contempt, applause and jeering, and so on, though manifestly responses persons are sometimes worthy of, are never treatments people are qualified for. Just as the winners in lotteries are entitled to their prizes but cannot be said to deserve them, so persons sometimes deserve praise or blame but are never entitled to them.
>
> (Feinberg 1970: 232)

The reason Feinberg gives for this is that there are no institutional rules that govern these informal responses. This means that there are no criteria the fulfilment of which would entitle you to receive admiration from others. At the very least, it is reasonable to think that cases where people are entitled to admiration will be far rarer than cases in which they are entitled to an honour.

The argument from desert, which is often taken by its proponents to conclusively show that we ought to honour and admire those who achieve great things, therefore in fact shows something much weaker than its proponents take it to show; namely, that we have some reason to do so but that these reasons may well be outweighed. These reasons will typically be stronger where the desert claim is also an entitlement claim. Honours governed by strict criteria are more likely to generate entitlement claims than other forms of honour. Admiration, on the other hand, will rarely, if ever, be something to which someone is entitled.

2 Moralism

There is something to the argument from desert, then, but only if it is understood to be a defeasible reason in favour of honouring and admiring those who have achieved excellent things but acted immorally. However, this raises the issue of whether the moral reasons against honour and admiration that we identified in the previous chapter could override the desert considerations that count in favour of honour and admiration. In other words, is the immorality of the person who has achieved excellent things the kind of consideration that should stop us from honouring and admiring them?

According to one common response to this question, the answer is no. Consider Agnès Poirier's (2010) claim that those who complain about honouring Polanski with awards are guilty of "prurient hounding" and "moralistic prejudices". Similarly, consider Heather MacDonald's criticism of those who cancelled performances by opera singer Plácido Domingo after a number of allegations of sexual harassment were made against him:

> It is a grotesque inversion of the proper hierarchy between public accomplishment and private sexual behavior to sacrifice an artist of Domingo's stature for the sake of 20 disgruntled bit players, laboriously harvested from thousands of professional interactions characterized by graciousness and consideration. Put simply, the discomfort of these belated accusers decades ago is not worth Domingo's head. Civilization rests on the realm of public achievement in ideas, politics, and art. The private realm of Eros should be subordinate to the public realm; how someone behaves in or getting to the bedroom is irrelevant to his achievements in the public square, absent criminality.
>
> (MacDonald 2019)

In other words, people should continue to honour and admire Domingo because his achievements are more important than his moral indiscretions.

In both of these examples, the behaviour of those who think we should not honour and admire artists in the light of morally objectionable behaviour is criticized for being overly judgemental or moralistic. The message is that we should not allow our moral judgements of those who have created great works of art to get in the way of our admiration for them. While this argument is usually made in relation to artists, similar arguments could be made for intellectuals and political figures who have achieved great things.

Here too it could be claimed that it would be moralistic to allow one's moral judgements to prevent an appreciation of their talents and achievements. In order to evaluate this argument, we need first to understand what moralism is and why it is a vice.[7]

Philosophers working on moralism have proposed various ways of understanding it. Craig Taylor (2012: 153) claims that moralism is "a failure to recognize what moral thought or reflection requires (and does not require) of us". According to Taylor, a purely judgemental response to another's wrongdoing is often not enough. We must also respond sympathetically and in a way that recognizes our common humanity. This involves having the correct emotional reactions to the person we are judging. Another way in which moralism can present itself according to Taylor (2012: Ch.4) is in allowing moral thought and judgement to extend their influence beyond their proper limits in our lives. Similarly, Julia Driver (2006: 37) claims that moralism is "the illicit introduction of moral considerations". In other words, there are some situations in which moral judgement is simply inappropriate, and moralism may involve a disposition to make moral judgements in these situations. What underlies both these forms of behaviour is that they involve an inflated sense of the extent to which moral criticism is appropriate.

There are at least two ways in which the moral criticism may be inappropriate. First, the criticism may not fit the behaviour being criticized. This may be because the behaviour being criticized is not morally wrong or because the person performing the act had an excuse for acting in a way that would otherwise be wrong or because the criticism is disproportionate to the wrongdoing.[8] Alternatively, criticism may be inappropriate due to features of the context in which the utterance is made rather than features of the behaviour being criticized. For example, to engage in extensive criticism of someone while delivering a eulogy may be inappropriate even if the criticisms fit the behaviour of the deceased.

What is the most plausible way to interpret the claim that it would be moralistic to allow one's moral judgements to prevent an appreciation of their talents? Different versions of this argument may well have different forms of moralism in mind when making this criticism. In some cases, the argument may be that moral criticism is inappropriate because the target did nothing wrong. For our purposes, these kinds of argument are less interesting, as we are interested in the ethics of honouring and admiring the immoral. This question does not arise for those who are deemed not to have acted immorally.

More interesting from our point of view are those who appeal to moralism while accepting that the behaviour itself was wrong and inexcusable. Those who defend Polanski, for example, tend not to argue that there is nothing wrong with raping a 13-year-old girl. Rather, the claim seems to be that allowing this wrongdoing to affect one's appreciation of Polanski's talent and achievements is inappropriate. In Poirier's defence of Polanski (2010), for example, she objects to the continued "hounding" of Polanski for a crime that took place 33 years ago. Here the claim seems to be that continuing to hold Polanski's crime against him is a *disproportionate* response to his wrongdoing.

Other defences of Polanski involve the idea that focusing on his wrongdoing is *inappropriate in certain contexts*. For example, in defence of the decision to make Polanski the chair of the Cesar awards, Aurélie Filippetti, a former French culture minister, said that Polanski is a

great director [...] who should be allowed to preside over this ceremony. It's something that happened 40 years ago. One cannot bring up this affair every time we talk about him because there was a problem back then. It is just an awards ceremony.

(Henley 2017)

Here the claim seems to be both that being influenced by Polanski's immoral behaviour would be both disproportionate to the crime (it "happened 40 years ago" after all) and that it would be the inappropriate context ("it is just an award ceremony").

A number of answers have been suggested to the question of why moralism should be viewed as a vice. Some see moralism as involving a violation of our moral requirements to others. For example, Robert Fullinwider (2006: 10–11) claims that morality requires us to be charitable towards other people's behaviour. Moralism is wrong, then, because it violates this duty to others. Relatedly, Kamila Pacovská (2018: 248) has argued that moralism is a failure of our duty "to exert an effort to love and accept the world such as it is, despite its imperfections". Others see moralism as damaging the moral character of the moralistic agent. C.A.J. Coady (2006: 25), for example, claims that moralism "can bring with it crippling psychological attitudes that themselves damage the operation of moral judgement". Finally, one of us (Archer 2018a) has argued that the problem with moralism is that it undermines the force of legitimate moral criticism.

We think that there is something to each of these claims about why moralism is wrong in general. However, these claims do not seem to really capture the moralism objection to letting our moral judgements influence how we view those who have achieved great things. MacDonald's defence of Domingo, for example, stresses the importance of not allowing public achievement to be undermined by the "private realm of Eros" because: "Civilisation rests on the realm of public achievement in ideas, politics, and art". The claim here is not that we are violating our moral duties to others, damaging our own moral character, or undermining the force of moral criticism. Rather, the claim is that we are undermining civilization itself!

While this claim strikes us as overblown, there is a reasonable point to be made here. According to Steven Jauss (2008: 255), moralism may deprive people of potentially valuable aesthetic and epistemic experiences. In responding in a moralistic way, we may close ourselves off to these valuable experiences. Jauss supports this claim with some lines from Stephen Dunn's *Moralists* in which the speaker claims:

> Whenever I've been one [a moralist], I've known the end of my thinking in advance, the door shut before it's opened wide enough to let in the ill wind, the rude, spectacular visage, the simple truth obstructed in a corner.
>
> (Dunn 1994: 24; cited in Jauss 2008: 255)

This point more closely captures MacDonald's claims about why we should not let our moral judgements cloud our appreciation of Domingo. In doing so, we would put obstacles in the way of our appreciation of valuable aesthetic experiences. A moralistic approach to Polanski may therefore prevent us from fully appreciating his cinematic achievements. This point is not limited to the artistic case. In taking a moralistic approach to an intellectual figure, we also run the risk of blocking an appreciation of their valuable intellectual achievements. Similarly, a moralistic approach to political figures may also run the risk of making us unable to appreciate the great things they have achieved.

It is not just the value of certain achievements that a moralistic attitude may close us off from. Moralism may also close us from seeing wrongdoers as fellow members of the moral community. As Linda Radzik observes, there is a "disturbing tendency to see the wrongdoer as the 'other', as a distinct kind of being who is different from ourselves, whom we presume to be perfectly responsive to the call of morality" (2009: 12). In doing so, we run the risk of failing to take wrongdoers seriously as moral agents and instead seeing them as beings "who must be handled in some way" (Radzik 2009: 3). One problem that may arise from being too quick to withdraw admiration in response to wrongdoing is that it may contribute to this tendency to see wrongdoers as distinct kinds of beings and in doing so fail to treat them seriously as moral agents.

In othering wrongdoers in this way, we may inadvertently help to support the great person myths we discussed in the previous chapter. As we explained, we uphold the myth that great people cannot be immoral when we hold that someone's great achievements justify or render tolerable the wrongs they might have committed. However, another way to feed this myth is to insist that those who perform immoral acts can never achieve great things. Refraining from ever honouring or admiring those who have acted immorally may also serve to reinforce the myth that those who achieve great things are also morally virtuous. If we want to undermine this myth, then it would be misguided to always withhold honour and admiration from the immoral.

Relatedly, as Alexis Shotwell (2016) points out, when responding to systematic forms of wrongdoing in which many people are complicit to varying degrees, many people have a tendency to respond by striving for personal purity. There are several problems with this response. First, it is unlikely to be achievable and so we will always end up disappointed. Second, striving for purity can produce "a seemingly satisfying self-righteousness" (Shotwell 2016: 203). This self-righteousness may get in the way of recognizing our own moral failings and our complicity in systematic wrongdoing. It may also get in the way of solidarity with others. Finally, as Mary Douglas (1966: 4) argues, the goal of purity is often "to impose system on an inherently untidy experience". In striving for purity, we therefore run the risk of simplifying a complicated and nuanced situation. There is a danger, then, that in striving to avoid honouring and admiring the immoral we may be pursuing a purity project that is doomed to failure, that will get in the way of solidarity and the recognition of our own failings, and that will lead to an overly simplistic moral outlook.

In summary, being overly judgemental in our approach to admiring and honouring the immoral could interfere with our appreciation of those who achieve great things and contribute to a simplistic moral outlook that fails to treat wrongdoers as members of the moral community. However, it would be a mistake to conclude from this that we should never respond to the moral reasons considered in the previous chapter by withholding honour and admiration. While we should be reluctant about being too eager to engage in moral criticism, this should not prevent us from engaging in moral criticism altogether. Being unwilling to ever morally criticize is no more a virtue than being too ready to do so. This would be to embody the opposite vice of moral indifference.

As with the argument from desert, the argument from moralism is taken by many to show conclusively that we ought to honour and admire those who achieve great things. However, what this argument actually supports is reason to be cautious about the extent to which admiration and honour are withheld for moral reasons and the wider projects to which this withholding may contribute. A major film organization that chooses never to honour or admire the immoral will likely miss out on directing people's attention towards some important and valuable artistic achievements. It may also contribute to a process of othering wrongdoers and be, or be perceived to be, part of a doomed purity project. However, a film organization that pays no attention to the moral reasons considered in the previous chapter risks empowering the wrongdoer, harming their victims, and perpetuating a damaging ideology. It is right to be wary of the dangers of moralism, but this does not justify turning our backs on morality altogether. In deciding whether or not to honour and admire the immoral we must judge whether there really are sufficient reasons to withhold honour and admiration or whether this would be a moralistic and overly judgemental response.

3 Distinctive Achievements of the Immoral

We have argued that an overly moralistic approach towards those who have achieved great things may interfere with our appreciation of their achievements. While this is an important worry, by itself it does not seem to provide an especially forceful reason to continue to honour and admire the achievements of the immoral or at least to continue to honour and admire them in the way we now do. While we may miss out on a full appreciation of great works of art, intellectual contributions, or political achievements if we do not admire the work of the immoral, we are unlikely to be left with a great shortage of things to admire. There are more great works of art, literature, and philosophy than we can ever hope to engage within one lifetime. In the words of Susan Wolf (2010: 47), most philosophy and most works of art and literature, even those that are excellent, are such "that it would have been no loss to the world if [they] had never been published". By this Wolf does not mean that these works have no value or that it would not be worth our while engaging with them. Rather, Wolf's point is that people would not be worse off if they instead engaged with some other equally valuable work.[9] Given this, it is not clear we will be worse off if we choose not to admire the achievements of those who have acted immorally, as there are plenty of other achievements to admire.[10]

There will be some exceptions to this argument. Some achievements will be irreplaceable. One way in which achievements may be irreplaceable is when they are so exceptionally brilliant that there is nothing of comparable value. If Polanski's *Chinatown* really is the best film of all time, as claimed by *The Guardian*, then something will be lost if someone chooses to admire the achievements of a different director instead. Similarly, for opera lovers there may be nothing that can compare to the work of Richard Wagner. In these cases, there will be something of value that is lost when we miss out on a full appreciation of these artists.

Similar arguments can be made about some scientific achievements. For example, the Pernkopf Anatomy of Man is a classic anatomy atlas that has been widely praised for its accuracy and detail (Riggs 1998). Other atlases are claimed by some surgeons to pale in comparison to Pernkopf's atlas (Begley 2019). For complex surgical procedures, then, it may be the most useful guide that surgeons have to navigating the human body. This atlas, though, was created in the 1930s by Viennese medical illustrators who were committed Nazis who even included images of swastikas in their signatures. Even worse, the drawings may have been based upon the bodies of those executed by the Nazi party (Yee et al. 2019). If we see the use of this atlas as a way of honouring its creators, albeit a rather minor form of honour, then there may be cases where providing the best medical care will involve honouring these committed Nazis. Again, then, we will lose something of value if we decide not to honour those who have created this work by continuing to use it to guide surgical procedures.

Nevertheless, the scope of this argument is necessarily limited. While there may be cases where we will miss out on something of great value if we do not engage with the works and achievements of the immoral, this only applies to works that are *exceptional*. In all other cases, we will not be worse off if we cannot fully appreciate the achievements of the immoral, as there will be plenty of other equally excellent achievements for us to appreciate.

There is, though, another way to argue that we would miss something important if we do not admire the achievements of the immoral. There may be distinctive contributions to life that can only be made by people who are morally flawed. According to this argument, we would miss important insights into the human condition if we were unable to fully appreciate these achievements. A version of this argument is suggested by Wills and Holt (2017). They claim that a capacity for moral imagination is, to some extent at least, a different skill from that of being a morally good person. While some degree of moral imagination may be necessary for being a good person, it is far from sufficient. Moreover, they even suggest that it is possible that an overdeveloped capacity for moral imagination may hinder the development of moral virtue. Given that moral imagination and moral virtue are separable, an artist may produce important works of moral imagination without being a virtuous person.

While we agree that this is a possibility, it does not by itself give us much by way of response to the claim that being unable to appreciate the achievements of the immoral would not make us worse off. Perhaps we would be missing out on some important feats of moral imagination, but, so long as there are other equally important works of moral imagination out there, this does not seem to make us any worse off. But there is a related argument that is capable of providing such a response.

In his book *Wagner: The Terrible Man and His Truthful Art*, Owen Lee attempts to understand how "a hateful, ranting man" committed to an "almost pathological anti-Semitism" (1999: 20, 15) could produce such extraordinary and indispensable operas. Lee's answer is that there is an important connection between Wagner's immorality and the brilliance of his art. To begin to see this, we must first consider what artworks are capable of achieving. Great art brings us pleasure, but Lee argues it is also able

> [to] deepen our awareness of the things that matter, to enable us to accept darkness and pain, to tell us what we might not have wanted to know but needed to know, to make us into something more than we were before, more human and more compassionate. And, most of all I think, to enable us to see into ourselves.
>
> (Lee 1999: 91)

In Lee's (1999: 91–92) view, it was Wagner's own inner conflict, "his wounded self", "demons", and "conflicting emotions" that made it possible for him to see "deeper into human nature than the rest of us are likely to do". It is for this reason that Lee thinks we need his work and the work by similarly troubled and troubling artists "to see unerringly into ourselves and so to help us with our lives" (Lee 1999: 92).

Barbara Leaming makes a related claim about the work of Polanski. According to Leaming (1982: 142), Polanski's brilliance as a director comes from his unique ability to examine the relationship between identity and self-presentation. His method for doing so is to engage in a "blatant theatricalisation of himself on screen" and it is this that "gives Polanski his singular but indisputable place in film history" (Leaming 1982: 142). Importantly for Leaming, Polanski's films cannot be fully understood without viewing them "against the vivid background of the director's autobiographical legend" (Leaming 1982: 142). And this legend is of a director who has escaped the horrors of the Holocaust and is fascinated by "the perspective offered by the chaos of war" and seeks to create art that "explores the limits of unbridled violence and desire" (Leaming 1982: 143). According to Leaming, it is this distinct perspective, unburdened by moral concern, that makes Polanski's work so ground-breaking. This image of amorality was one that Polanski was unable to control after his trial for the rape of Samantha Geimer, and many of his subsequent films are responses to this inability to control his public image.[11] In Leaming's words:

> His is a peculiarly modern tale, one possible only in an age of mass media and information. Having set out to create an image for himself – an artistic identity – he became a public effect, to which his art was now pressed to respond.
>
> (Leaming 1982: 144)

Polanski's films may therefore be important in part for the discomfort caused by their amoral perspective. Moreover, the distinct perspective offered by Polanski's later films arises in part from the way Polanski's own immoral behaviour and the public reaction to it has shaped his perspective. If you were unable to appreciate Polanski's achievements, and the achievements of other artists whose work is informed by an amoral perspective or the artist's own immorality, then you would close yourself off from important insights into the human condition.

You therefore have good reason not to turn your back completely on the works and achievements of the immoral. These may be exceptionally valuable and irreplaceable or offer important insights into the human condition that are only available from their perspective. Again, though, this is far from a conclusive reason to think that people ought to honour and admire the creator of such works. These reasons have to be considered alongside the reasons that count against honour and admiration that we explored in the previous chapter. In deciding whether the kinds of reasons we have identified in this section are present for any particular case, you should ask yourself whether the works and achievements are truly exceptional or irreplaceable for some other reason. More generally, when considering whether or not to abandon admiration for the immoral, you should ask whether in refusing to admire those who have acted immorally you might be shutting yourself off from distinctive contributions and insights into the human condition. As we argue in the next chapter, even if these works are exceptional, you might still be able to appreciate and even honour and admire works without honouring and admiring their creators.

4 Personal Value

Michele Wallace (1990: 85) argues that Michael Jackson's music videos provide an important commentary on black American experience that constitutes a form of "black modernism" that challenges "conventional hierarchies of class, race, sexuality, and aesthetic mastery". Against a background of the cultural marginalization of black Americans, Wallace (1990: 88) describes how the video for Jackson's song *Bad* represents a subversive struggle for "aesthetic, professional, sexual, and racial independence". Wallace's admiration for Jackson was also informed by her relationship with her mother, the artist Faith Ringgold, who had created a quilt devoted to Jackson's *Bad* to be sold at a benefit auction for Bishop Desmond Tutu. In Ringgold's view what Jackson's song shows is that the badness that Jackson is referring to is the "struggle for space" that marginalized groups have to fight for in order to achieve any kind of cultural representation. The people who are classed as bad, according to Ringgold, are those who "defy very destructive forces in order to help not only themselves but other people" (cited in Wallace 1990: 89). Wallace's appreciation for Jackson, then, is informed both by the work Jackson has done to open up cultural space for black Americans and her relationship with her mother.

Wallace's essay was written long before allegations of Jackson's sexual abuse of children came to light. Nevertheless, the point she makes here is important for our purposes. Jackson's work is simply not replaceable for Wallace, as her appreciation of it is intimately connected to her identity. This includes both her identity as a black American and her identity as the daughter of the artist Faith Ringgold.

A related point can be found in Maxfield Sparrow's defence of autistic people who continue to define themselves as having Asperger's syndrome:

> While I still don't personally want to be called an Aspie, I am ready to fight on behalf of my Autistic siblings who do connect with that identity [...] as a cultural marker of their understanding of themselves and the world we live in.
>
> (Sparrow and Silberman 2018)

Sparrow's point is that the role the labels "Asperger's syndrome" and "Aspie" have played in the lives of some autistic people justifies the continued use of these terms. Even though these labels may be seen to honour Hans Asperger, a man complicit in the murder of autistic children (Sheffer 2018), the importance of these labels to the identity of some autistic people means that they should be free to continue using them.

A similar concern is also raised against the removal of confederate statues in the USA. In the words of the National Trust for Historic Preservation (2017), these statues "were intended as a celebration of white supremacy when they were constructed". Moreover, "they are still being used as symbols and rallying points for such hate today".[12] Nevertheless, some who accept that these statues honour and memorialize racist people claim that they should not be removed. According to Demetriou and Wingo (2018), the fact that these figures are viewed as heroic by a significant group of people gives us reason not to remove them. In their words, "Every people needs its heroes" (Demetriou and Wingo 2018: 351) and by removing these statues we would be depriving white southerners of their ancestral heroes. They argue that white southerners may admire the sacrifices and loyalty of those who fought for the confederacy without condoning their entire political outlook (Demetriou and Wingo 2018: 352). The fact that these people fought for the group they belong to may give white southerners special reason to honour them, as this is a core part of their cultural history. The claim that removing statues would be erasing history may be understood as expressing a community's desire to continue to admire and honour their ancestral heroes who have helped to shape their group identity.[13]

In addition, some people may feel personal attachment to the statue as an object rather than to what it represents. Statues often serve as meeting points, and someone may have fond memories of meeting their partner there on a first date. Others may remember walking past the statue every day on their way to work and being glad to have something interesting and familiar to look at. In these cases, the statue as an object has a value that is not easily replaceable, as it comes from the historical connection people have to the object.

The basic thought we can take from all these examples is that the role that someone's actions or achievements has played in shaping one's identity may provide additional reasons to continue to honour and admire that person. This means that there will be something lost for people who are unable to continue appreciating these achievements or using these labels, even if other equally valuable work or equally useful labels are available. These claims can be justified by appealing to the existence of personal value. According to Gerry Cohen (2013: 167–169), our personal connections with particular objects can give us reason to value those objects more than we would other objects that are just as valuable, or even more so, from an impersonal point of view.[14] In Cohen's case, an eraser that he had used throughout his academic career was far more valuable to him than any other eraser could ever be, no matter how much more valuable that eraser would be from an impersonal point of view. The reason Cohen (2013: 168) gives to explain why objects can acquire this kind of value, which he calls personal value, is that we have a "need to *belong* to something". We achieve this in part by preserving things that are part of our past. We can think of this as a desire to be part of what Edmund Burke (1999: 96 cited in Cohen 2013: 168) called the "partnership not only between those who are living, but between those who are living, those who are dead, and those who are to be born".

Accepting the existence of personal value provides an additional reason to think that at least some people have good reason to continue to honour and admire the work of the immoral. For those whose identities have been shaped in a significant way by Michael Jackson's music, his musical achievements cannot simply be replaced by those of other people. Even if the other music is equally valuable from an impersonal point of view, it will not have the same personal connections as Jackson's music has for Wallace. It will not have played the same important role in her personal biography or in shaping the collective identity of black Americans. Similarly, for those whose identity has been significantly shaped by the label Aspie, abandoning this label for one that is equally valuable from an impersonal point of view may involve significant loss. Those whose lives and identities have been significantly shaped by the achievements of the immoral may then have additional reason to continuing to admire and honour these achievements. Again, though, this reason has to be understood as a defeasible one. Giving up something of personal value is hard; it is also something that we can sometimes be morally required to do. For example, because confederate statues are upholding and reinforcing a white supremacist ideology, in many cases they should be removed, even though these statues have personal value for some people. Of course, some may disagree about our judgement in this case; the important point for our argument here is that the mere fact that some people have reason to continue to honour and admire the work or actions of the immoral does not provide a decisive reason to honour and admire them. Rather, it is a reason that may be outweighed by the reasons that count against honour and admiration.

5 How to Respond?

In Chapters 1 and 2, we argued that the immoral can be admirable. So, we can have (fittingness) reasons to honour and admire the immoral. In Chapter 3, we considered three general reasons against honouring and admiring the immoral. In this chapter, we have outlined four general reasons in favour of honouring and admiring the immoral. Importantly, we have argued that none of the reasons we have considered are in general decisive. This allows that they may be decisive in particular cases, but the particular details of each case must typically be considered to figure that out. Once you have established a person is a fitting target of admiration, and then considered the weight of the reasons against, you must then weigh these against the reasons for honouring and admiring the immoral.

First, you must ask: does the person *deserve* to be admired? Those who create great artworks, make ground-breaking contributions to intellectual life, or shape a society's history in positive ways generally deserve to be honoured and admired. As a result, there is generally good reason to honour and admire them. The fact the person deserves admiration gives you a stronger reason to admire them than if they were just a fitting target of admiration.

Second, is the immoral person entitled to an honour or admiration? If an award has clear and precise criteria governing who should receive it, then the person who meets these criteria is likely to be entitled to the award. For example, in a 100-metre sprint race, the winner is the person who crosses the finish line first without breaking any of the relevant rules. This is a clear case where someone is entitled to the prize, which means that they have a right to it. An entitlement claim then generally provides a stronger reason to ensure someone receives an honour than a desert claim. However, even these claims might be overridden in exceptional circumstances. There may even be occasions when someone is entitled to feelings of admiration.

Third, do you have any responsibility to ensure an immoral person gets the honour and admiration they deserve or are entitled to? Recall that the fact that someone deserves honour and admiration does not mean that it is your responsibility to ensure that they receive this; nor does the fact that a person is entitled to an honour mean that you must give it to them. Those with no interest in cinema may have little or no reason to ensure that Polanski is admired for his talents as a filmmaker. Similarly, those left cold by opera have little reason to ensure that Wagner is honoured and admired. On the other hand, an awards committee deciding who should receive the best director award has a far greater responsibility to ensure that filmmakers receive the honour and admiration they deserve. If it is your responsibility to ensure someone gets the honour and admiration they deserve or are entitled to, then you will have a much stronger reason to honour and admire them.

Fourth, are you giving too much weight to moral reasons or responding in a way that is disproportional to the wrongdoing? In other words, are you being moralistic? The most relevant charge of moralism in this context is that being moralistic leads to people closing themselves off from valuable experiences. So, when considering a particular case of honouring or admiring someone who has acted immorally, people should consider whether they may be operating with an inflated sense of the appropriateness of moral criticism and are losing out on valuable experiences as a result. We should also consider if we are engaging in a misguided search for moral purity. This is unlikely to be an easy question to answer, as there is no simple way to determine whether one is giving too much weight to moral concerns or responding in a way that is disproportional to the wrongdoing. Nevertheless, it is important to bear in mind that moral reasons are not the only reasons to consider when deciding how to respond to any particular case. We should also consider the aesthetic and epistemic reasons we may have to admire great artists, intellectuals, and historical figures.

Fifth, are the person's achievements truly exceptional? While there are many achievements that can be replaced, there are some works that cannot be replaced with other achievements. For example, you might have to honour and admire Einstein for his discoveries in physics because you cannot have a good understanding of contemporary physics without doing so.

Finally, has an immoral person and their achievements played an important role in shaping your identity? If so, then this might justify your continuing to honour and admire that person even when there are good moral reasons that count against doing so. Of course, there are times when this will not be the case. Sometimes you will have to take the damage to your identity that ceasing to honour and admire would imply. Even so, it is still a relevant consideration in favour of honouring and admiring an immoral person.

Having identified all the relevant reasons, you must then weigh up what you should actually do. You might find that you have decisive reasons against. Or you might find that you have decisive reasons in favour of honouring and admiring. While there can be decisive reasons in favour of either abandoning admiration or doing nothing and continuing to honour and admire the immoral, the fact the reasons we have identified are not decisive in all cases undermines any attempt to give a general policy on how we ought to respond to these figures. This may make the decision-making process messier than some might hope for. There will often not be clear reasons in favour of either abandoning or doing nothing. Sometimes you will have to try a middle-ground approach. Sometimes you will have to try to honour and admire while avoiding the moral dangers we have identified. In the next chapter, we consider various ways we might focus admiration so that we can avoid these dangers.

Notes

1 The idea that people ought to get what they deserve is a popular idea, at least according to Aristotle (*Nicomachean Ethics* Book V), who claims that "all men agree that what is just in distribution must be according to desert in some sense". Similarly, David Schmidtz (2002: 774) claims that this idea is one that "most people believe", even if "philosophers often say otherwise".

2 For relevant debate about the relationship between fittingness and desert, see, for example, Carlsson (2017) and Macnamara (2020).

3 See Olsaretti (2003: 4–8) for a helpful overview of theories of the bases of desert.

4 There may be other emotional bases for commemorative statues. For example, gratitude for someone's service. As Feinberg (1970: 228–229)

points out, gratitude can also be the emotional basis for deserving an award.

5 We might understand this claim as holding a prima facie duty to ensure people get what they deserve. This way of understanding the claim will be in line with the weakened version of the claim we offer below.

6 Another way to support this claim would be to argue, as Olsaretti (2003: 8) does, that the force of desert is not always deontic but rather sometimes telic and sometimes deontic. If we accept this view of desert, then the fact that someone deserves something does not imply that anyone else has an obligation to bring it about that they receive what they deserve.

7 The following paragraphs draw heavily on Archer (2018a).

8 See Archer (2018a: 343–344) for a more extensive explanation of the possibilities here.

9 Similar points are made by Archer and Matheson (2019b: 18) and Liao (2017).

10 This point should not be confused with the claim that we should only admire the works and achievements of the morally perfect. As Wolf (1982) points out elsewhere, the traits required to be morally perfect are likely in tension with those required to dedicate oneself to creating great works of art, literature, or, indeed, any non-moral achievement.

11 In an interview about his 2019 film *J'Accuse* (English title: *An Officer and a Spy*) about the wrongful conviction of Alfred Dreyfus, Polanski claimed that he drew on his own experience of being the subject of public scorn in making the film. He claimed: "I am familiar with many of the workings of the apparatus of persecution shown in the film, and that has clearly inspired me" (Bradley 2019).

12 See Burch-Brown (2017) for further discussion of the way in which statues can be used to uphold white supremacist ideology. See also Burch-Brown (forthcoming).

13 Alternatively, as Daniel Abrahams (forthcoming) argues, we may understand this claim that taking down statues amounts to erasing history as the view that the subject of the statue was objectively important to the shaping of a group identity. On this view, the defence of these statues is not about defending the character of the person depicted but rather about defending a particular view of the group's identity.

14 As Camil Golub (2019: 79) argues, accepting this kind of approach to valuing particular objects or past decisions, relationships, or projects can be thought of as an extension of the view that we can value certain things in a privileged way because of our relationship to them.

5   Refocusing Admiration

We have identified reasons for and against honouring and admiring the immoral. Neither set of reasons supports a general policy, but it is sometimes appropriate to do nothing and sometimes appropriate to abandon admiration. But what should you do if you determine that you cannot do nothing and cannot abandon admiration? In this chapter, we outline three approaches that become options once doing nothing and abandoning are off the table.

Before we consider these approaches, we first identify a reason why both approaches fail as general policies and then use this reason to guide the subsequent approaches that we outline in this chapter. In Section 1, we will argue that they fail as policies because they both encourage or manifest the *vice of globalism* – that is, they both involve conceiving of people in simplistic and reductive ways that are both inaccurate and morally dangerous. So, other approaches ought to avoid encouraging or manifesting this vice.

In Section 2, we outline the focused-admiration approach. This involves honouring and admiring immoral people by focusing on their admirable traits and achievements and in ways that do not imply they are thoroughly admirable people. We then consider a narrower version of the focused admiration approach in Section 3. When we cannot admire the person's traits, perhaps we should just honour and admire their *achievements*. In other words, we should separate the achievement from the person. We discuss when and why this approach is not an appropriate option – in particular, when we cannot in principle or in practice separate the achievement from the person. We then consider an option that applies when all other options seem impermissible – namely, the ambiguity approach. In contrast with the focused-admiration approach (in its general and separating forms), the ambiguity approach places greater emphasis on the person's immorality and acknowledges the difficulty of practically separating it from what makes the person admirable.

DOI: 10.4324/9780367810153-5

This has a moral benefit: you can gain insight into the workings of immorality. However, it also has moral drawbacks.

1 The Vice of Globalism

Recall that we earlier rejected globalism about admiration, the view that admiration involves an implicit assessment of the *whole* person. We did not go into detail about the forms that this assessment can take because we argued that there is no good reason to endorse globalism about admiration. However, there are two conceptions of globalism that are relevant here.

Perhaps the strongest form of globalism about admiration holds that it involves judging that the person is purely admirable. This precludes the admirable also being immoral. Another form of globalism about admiration holds that admiration involves judging that a person's admirable achievements and traits are *more important* than their immoral behaviour and non-admirable traits (Bell 2011). While we think that the latter kind of view is more plausible than the former kind, we do not think that either view is particularly plausible. As we argued in Chapter 2, there are no good arguments in favour of admiration being globalist.

We do not raise these views here to assess them, but rather to suggest that these two kinds of global assessment are in fact forms of a moral-epistemic vice. We manifest this vice when we conceive of people in simplistic and reductive ways. For example, when we identify a person with or reduce a person to a trait or an action of theirs. We in effect treat the person as if they are *just* the immoral trait or action. Note that making a global assessment of a person is not vicious. Our point is that those who manifest the vice of globalism will mistakenly exclusively focus, or place greater importance, on one side of a person. In effect, those who manifest this vice *globalize* an aspect of a person. This can involve taking the person's immorality to render everything else about them irrelevant or non-existent.

The vice of globalism is not just manifested when a person's immorality is treated this way. It is manifested whenever a trait or action has this automatically dominating effect in our assessment of a person. For example, we might take a great artist's aesthetic traits and achievements to automatically dominate our assessment of them. They will be identified with or reduced to these aesthetically virtuous traits and excellent achievements. Notice that this is related to what we earlier called *great person myths*. One of these myths is that a person's greatness is incompatible with their being immoral. The great artist, then, cannot be immoral. Another of these myths is that a person's greatness is more important than their immorality. Notice that both forms of this myth are manifestations of the vice of globalism. In both cases, we reduce a person to, or identify a person with, a particular trait or achievement. The tendency to think of people in this way is wrong in part because it is generally inaccurate. People are not in general reducible to or identifiable with a particular trait or action. Rather, they possess many traits and perform many different actions. To put it more casually, we are a messy mix of good and bad traits, of egoism and altruism, of caring and uncaring. We are rarely just one thing.[1] There may be times when it is justified to reduce a person to a particular action – for example, when the action is so extraordinarily wrong. But globalizing should only be done in exceptional cases. We manifest the vice when we globalize beyond exceptional cases, and we manifest it to a greater degree the more we globalize in our evaluations of people.

The problem for both the do-nothing approach and the abandoning approach as general policies is that they manifest the vice of globalism and so support great person myths, albeit from different directions. If everyone always did nothing, no one would ever respond to any of the moral reasons against honouring and admiring the immoral. Among other things, this would at least implicitly support the idea that greatness at least outweighs – that is, is more important than – immorality. It may even at times explicitly support the idea that greatness is incompatible with immorality. According to this way of thinking, there are no admirable yet immoral people, because such people's greatness makes what would otherwise be immoral not immoral. While you might sometimes be justified in doing nothing, doing nothing as a general policy is impermissible because it supports the idea that greatness is incompatible with immorality or that the person's greatness is more important than their immorality.

It might seem that abandoning admiration does not support great person myths because it explicitly advocates *not* honouring and admiring those great people who are also immoral. The problem is that never honouring and admiring such immoral people still implicitly supports great person myths.

First, it can support the myth that greatness is incompatible with immorality. As we discussed in Chapter 4, Kate Manne objects to the conditional: if a person is great, then they are not immoral.

Manne (2017: 180) suggests we should reverse this reasoning: a person is immoral, so they are not great. Unlike Manne, we think that the conditional itself is the problem. It manifests the vice of globalism and upholds a great person myth. So, rather than reverse this conditional, we should instead get comfortable with the messy reality that great people are sometimes immoral and the immoral are sometimes great people. Thinking that greatness and immorality are incompatible manifests the vice of globalism because it supports a simplistic conception of a person as just one aspect of themselves (e.g. their greatness, their immorality) or reducible to one aspect of themselves (e.g. their greatness, their immorality).

Second, abandoning admiration can support the myth that a person's immorality is always more important than their greatness. This does seem like a less objectionable idea than the claim that a person's greatness is more important than their immorality. However, it is still objectionable because it also supports a simplistic view of people. People may not be literally identified or reduced to one aspect of themselves, but they will always be tarred by their immorality. Nothing they can do will ever be valued because of the wrong things they have done. We may of course point to cases where this should be the case. Sometimes a person's immorality does outweigh anything great they have done. But the fact we sometimes should do this does not mean we always or even typically should.

It is not only generally inaccurate to globalize but also morally dangerous. It might seem justifiable to replace one inaccurate view of people (e.g. great people cannot be immoral; great people's greatness is more important than their immorality) with another (e.g. the immoral cannot be great; a person's immorality is more important than her greatness). However, we have not destroyed great person myths by turning them on their heads. We are simply finding new ways to approach it. Great person myths rely, we submit, on what we have called the vice of globalism: the pernicious tendency to think of people in simplistic and reductive ways. Just as great person myths support harmful ideologies, the *inverted* great person myths also do so. Both reinforce a simplistic and reductive way of thinking about people, a way of thinking which seems to support harmful ideologies. If the inverted great person myths were to become the dominant social script of how we understand and engage with great but immoral people, then we would systematically discount the achievements of the immoral. Our minds might only imagine that the worst immoral people will be globalized and discounted, but it does not seem that the inverted great person myths are sensitive to this. Indeed, most of us are immoral to some extent so it risks that our wrongs end up being globalized and becoming what defines each of us as a person. And even with the worst people, you should still be open to the possibility that they can redeem themselves, or even just open to the possibility that they are not thoroughly bad people. Again, we do think there are exceptional cases in which we can permissibly globalize. But these should be exceptional cases and not something built into our social scripts or schemas.

Even though they are sometimes permissible options, both doing nothing and abandoning admiration are not good general policies. As policies, they encourage and manifest the vice of globalism and in so doing support the related great person myths. In short, these policies support a simplistic and morally dangerous view of people that ultimately involves the idea that people should be identified with or reduced to either their greatness or their immorality. In the rest of the chapter, we will consider approaches that aim to avoid manifesting the vice of globalism.

2 Focused Admiration

Suppose you find that you should not abandon honouring and admiring an immoral person, and you also find that should not maintain the status quo of honouring and admiring as we currently do (i.e. do nothing). What should you do? One option that we will outline in this section is that you should consider whether you can *focus* your admiration on the person in a way that avoids the moral dangers of doing nothing and abandoning admiration. A source of inspiration for this approach comes from Earl Spurgin's (2012) claim that we should not see role models as general exemplars – that is, as people all of whose behaviour should be emulated – but rather as exemplars for particular *qualities*. For example, we should only consider athletes to be athletic exemplars and not also moral exemplars. Athletes are good at sport and should be role models for sporting performance and nothing else. Role models, then, should only be emulated for their behaviour and traits in particular roles. The focused-admiration approach builds on a suggestion implicit in Spurgin's claim: you should make extremely clear that you honour and admire people for their admirable traits and achievements, and nothing else. The immoral should therefore not be honoured and admired in ways that imply honour and admiration for, or could be understood as honouring and admiring, their immoral traits or behaviour. Extra effort must be made, then, to avoid admiration spreading.

Another way of putting this proposal is to say that if we want to continue to admire the immoral then we need to engage in *moral decoupling*. This is what Bhattacharjee et al. (2013: 1169) call the process by which people separate their judgements about a person's immoral behaviour from their judgements about their non-moral performance. In a series of lab studies, they investigated how participants responded to vignettes about high-performing public figures who had acted immorally. They found that some participants responded to these vignettes by condoning actions they might normally condemn (moral rationalization strategies) but that others responded by separating their evaluation of the person's performance from their evaluation of their moral conduct (moral decoupling). Moreover, they found that it was possible to influence how participants responded to these vignettes by asking them to read statements encouraging one of these approaches (Bhattacharjee et al. 2013: 1171–1172). This suggests that this kind of focused admiration is possible and that it is possible to encourage it in others.

As we discussed earlier, many do take certain honours to be merely about particular admirable traits and achievements. The Oscars, for example, seems to be merely about aesthetic traits and achievements. There are two points to consider here. First, not all forms of honouring are so specific. Second, even specific forms of honouring can have adverse public meanings.

Consider statues that are placed on pedestals in prominent locations. Such statues honour the person who is depicted. In doing so, they pick out the person as admirable. As discussed in Chapter 3, this is partly because prominent locations are of high value and so they are prioritized for those deemed worthy of the attention of many people. As a result, it seems that the person is picked out as globally admirable. It is hard to identify the particular wrongs that a person has done if you also choose to create a glorifying permanent display of them in a place where many people will see them. The attention that will be drawn to the person is hard to understand as anything other than a global endorsement of the person. Even if a plaque is installed in an attempt to contextualize the statue, others will still see the person more prominently than the plaque.[2] Even if the plaque helps to show that the person has behaved immorally and this is taken seriously, it still suggests that the person's greatness is at least more important than their immorality. Either way, it seems that such statues manifest the vice of globalism and support great person myths. So, such statues do not seem to be acceptable forms of focused admiration.

This does not mean that statues are always impermissible. First, following Rossi (2020), we can distinguish between the ethics of putting statues in place and the ethics of taking down statues. Perhaps bad statues should be kept for reasons of social cohesion (Demetriou and Wingo 2018). Perhaps we can build statues depicting scenes because they can better focus admiration on a depicted person's admirable qualities (perhaps because they can better depict a more complicated narrative). As statues of people will often encourage or manifest the vice of globalism because they do not easily permit focused admiration, we think that statues will more often be the wrong way to honour a person.

Lifetime achievement awards are another type of honour that seem to involve a global endorsement of the person. Even so, such awards have an easier time adding nuance and de-globalizing contextual detail than a statue. A lifetime achievement award for an immoral filmmaker, for example, might include a discussion of the person's wrongs. This will be more justifiable if the person has redeemed themselves and apologized for what they did. But it may still be possible if the immoral person has not done this. Of course, though, an immoral person might not agree to receive such an award if it involves acknowledging wrongs they had not themselves acknowledged through regret, apology, and redemption.[3] Even so, setting aside legal challenges, this way of giving this kind of award might be a promising one. It would make clear that the person has done important things (whether in sport, art, politics, science, or elsewhere), but that their wrongs must also be commented upon – and indeed the person ought to be blamed for these wrongs.

More specific awards – such as an award for best director – do not seem to involve a global endorsement of the person. A person is being awarded for a specific thing – such as being the best director for a film released in the past year – rather than the award commenting on the importance or value of them as a person. Of course, such awards are currently given in a such a way that might be justifiably understood as – that is, having the public meaning of – giving a global endorsement of the person. Given that this is a problem of public meaning, it is something that can arguably be changed by changing how such awards are given.

One idea is to suspend the giving of an award to a person if there are outstanding allegations of serious wrongdoing against the winner, as the British Academy of Film and Television Arts

(BAFTA) did in 2019 with *Bohemian Rhapsody* director Bryan Singer. While his film remained nominated, Singer was not among the makers of the film that were cited on the nomination. The reasons they gave for doing so were "recent very serious allegations" of behaviour that BAFTA considers "completely unacceptable and incompatible with its values" (BAFTA 2019). By suspending this award, BAFTA both acknowledged the seriousness of the allegations and highlighted that one can deserve to win an award and yet be an immoral person. There remain worries about how such an award will be interpreted more widely and whether award-giving bodies might be accused of paying only superficial attention to the (alleged) wrongdoings of the awardee. Even so, we think that such awards can be given *if* award-giving bodies work hard to focus on the ways an awardee is being picked out as admirable.

Other honours might instead focus on the input of other people in bringing about an admirable achievement. A film award might draw more attention to all the people involved in the making of the film. After all, films are a collective effort involving hundreds and sometimes thousands of people. Even films with a single credited director often have other directors for different filming units. Even when a single person is credited with writing a film, they have often received input from others. In recognizing a great film such as Polanski's *Chinatown* you might seek to spread your admiration beyond the director and leading actors towards the hundreds of other people who worked on it. From the producers, scriptwriters, and editors to the runners, researchers, and accountants. Similarly, in recognizing someone's scientific achievements you could tell a story that focuses less on a single genius and more on the social context in which the discovery was made and the lab assistants, collaborators, and support staff who helped to bring about the discovery. Moving the admiration away from individuals and towards groups may also help to reduce the risk of admiration becoming a globalized response to an individual and instead a response to the qualities that helped to contribute to an outstanding achievement.

Political honours might do something similar. While Winston Churchill deserves to be admired for his role in defeating the Nazis, we should perhaps also focus on the importance of other people in this effort. Of course, political honours sometimes take the form of statues that focus on a particular individual, which we argued above was objectionable as they typically manifest the vice of globalism. Other political honours do not fare better: Churchill is featured on British pound notes. For a figure that is already very well known, he is granted the honour of being a feature of many cash transactions. Depiction on currency might be an appropriate honour for lesser-known figures so that others may learn about them. However, because Churchill is already so well known, depicting him on banknotes further supports a global assessment of him as admirable. Political honours may then need to be less permanent in order to properly focus admiration. Churchill, for example, could be honoured during remembrance ceremonies, and such ceremonies could discuss both his achievements and his wrongs during the war.[4] Such ceremonies could emphasize the efforts of everyone in defeating in the Nazis, as well as all the unjustified (or at least morally questionable) actions that occurred during the Second World War on each side. For example, the firebombing of Dresden, the Bengal famine, the dropping of multiple nuclear bombs on major Japanese cities should also be acknowledged alongside the bombing of Pearl Harbour, the Holocaust, and so-called comfort women forced into sexual slavery.

A general source of resistance to focused admiration is that it cuts against our honouring and admiring practices. According to Daniel Boorstin (1961: 43), a key element of celebrity culture is treating celebrities as heroes to be worshipped. While Boorstin (1961) claims that this is a new phenomenon and that in the past people celebrated real heroes, this strikes us as questionable. Celebrities are people whose ways of life capture our interest and attention not just for their skills or achievements but also for who they are (van Krieken 2012: 10). A culture of celebrity encourages a global form of admiration for those who become famous. Earlier forms of "hero culture" seem to be rudimentary forms of celebratory culture. Such hero and celebrity cultures seem quite engrained, so while we think that focusing admiration is one way to improve these practices, we should not dismiss the difficulty we will have in improving these practices. Indeed, there are powerful interests that are served by these cultures. Once someone is a celebrity their name can be used to sell products, to generate interest, and to direct attention (Rein et al. 1997: 15). Moreover, when a person is considered a hero, they can be used to support particular causes. The person can even become an embodiment of the cause. This presents an obstacle for attempts to encourage more focused forms of admiration, because any attempt to do so is likely to clash with those who have an interest in maintaining hero and celebrity culture. This is especially likely to be a problem in relation to art, sport, and entertainment. However, celebrity culture also plays a significant role in politics (Street 2004;

Archer et al. 2020) and academia (Walsh and Lehmann 2019). We suspect that for this approach to be fully successful there would need to be a wider societal change in the way people respond to fame and celebrity. We return to this point in the conclusion.

The focused-admiration approach will be especially difficult in cases where the admired person's talents are closely connected to their immoral behaviour. For example, it may be that Gauguin's artistic talents are tightly related to his immoral traits and actions (even if they are in principle separable). It might then be hard to separate honour and admiration for Gauguin with honour and admiration for his immorality. This is supported by Bhattacharjee et al.'s (2013) research on moral decoupling. They found that it is more difficult for people to separate their moral judgements about a person from their evaluation of that person's performance when the wrongdoing was closely related to their high performance. In fact, later research by Lee and Kwak (2016) found that participants often engage in what they call *moral coupling* in such cases – that is, people integrate their judgements of a person's moral conduct with their judgements of their performance. However, even in cases where the immoral behaviour is unrelated to the performance, such as a high-performing athlete who evades his taxes, people could be prompted to engage in moral coupling by reading statements encouraging this approach (Lee and Kwak 2016: 104–105). This suggests that the extent to which people are likely to separate someone's achievements from their immorality is influenced both by the connection between the achievement and the immorality and on whether or not they are encouraged to view these as separable.

In the next section, we consider the prospects of another form of the focused-admiration approach. Rather than focusing on the person's admirable traits *and* achievements, we focus instead entirely on their achievements. In so doing, we aim to *separate the achievement from the person*.

3 The Separating Approach

Can you instead simply focus on an immoral person's achievements? In the case of artworks, this suggestion is often put in terms of *separating the art from the artist*. You can also ask the following. Can we separate the athletic feat from the athlete? Can we separate the political view from the politician? Can we separate the scientific discovery from the scientist? These are more specific versions of the general suggestion that we can *separate the achievement*

from the person. Whenever you face an immoral person who has achieved something excellent, you can ask: can we honour and admire the achievement without honouring and admiring the person? We outline when this approach is possible in principle and identify challenges to it in practice.

This approach presupposes that an achievement is a distinct entity from the person responsible for it (Wills and Holt 2017). One immediate problem for this way of supporting the separating approach is that achievements and those responsible for them are not always distinct entities. Performance art pieces feature the artist as part of the performance (Nannicelli 2020: 51). Athletic feats necessarily involve the athlete. And so on. Because the person is an essential *part* of the achievement, it may be that you cannot honour and admire the achievement without honouring and admiring the person responsible for it. However, when we honour and admire these kinds of achievement, we at best honour and admire the person *as a feature* of the achievement. This is arguably quite different from honouring and admiring them *as a person* (for this achievement). It remains to be seen whether this line of argument is successful. If it is not, then the separating approach is not an option in cases where the person is part of their achievement.

Even in cases where the person is not part of their achievement, there are three kinds of link between a person and their achievement that may pose a problem for the separating approach. The first is that there is a *responsibility* link between a person and their achievement. This means that even if a person and their achievement are distinct entities, the person is still connected to their achievement in virtue of being responsible for it. This may pose a problem for focusing on the achievement alone because it may seem that by honouring and admiring an achievement you are still honouring and admiring the person responsible for it. However, it is not clear whether such *indirect* honour and admiration will have the moral dangers that directly honouring and admiring an immoral person has. If you honour and admire the theory of relativity, this would not carry the same moral dangers as it would if you honour and admire Albert Einstein: he, it has been claimed, harboured sexist and racist attitudes at least at some points in his life (Phillips 2018).

One reason why the theory of relativity can be honoured and admired without being morally dangerous is that it does not manifest any of Einstein's morally bad attitudes. We might therefore face moral dangers when there is an *attitude* link between an immoral person and an achievement of theirs. However, as with honouring and admiring achievements that feature the immoral person (e.g. performances), whether honouring and admiring an achievement is morally dangerous depends on what aspects of the achievement are being honoured and admired. While it may have an adverse public meaning to honour and admire an achievement that manifests, for example, racist attitudes, there is no reason to think we must honour and admire the racist attitude when we honour and admire the achievement.

Instead, it matters what the attitudes *do*. Perhaps attitudes contribute to an achievement through having an objectionable *meaning*. For example, when we learn that the Marquis de Sade likely acted out the brutality he depicts in *Justine* and *120 Days of Sodom*, this affects what those works mean. And you might worry that when you admire those works, you are honouring and admiring Sade's immorality. But it is not the meaning of these works that we think results in its never being possible to separate those artworks from the artist. If you endorse a strong view of artwork meaning such that it is up to each person to decide what an artwork means to them (e.g. Barthes 1967; though see Grady 2019), then the meaning you give an immoral artist's work can be completely unconnected to their real-life immorality – for example, you might find a feminist message in de Sade's work. Instead, we propose that separation is not possible when achievements (which include artworks) have a dubious *moral function* – namely, that of justifying, excusing, or condoning the wrongs of the immoral person responsible for them.[5] When an achievement has this function, it is not possible to separate the achievement from the person's immorality.

Wills and Holt (2017) allude to this view when they write that the Marquis de Sade's *Justine* and *120 Days of Sodom* acted as "an implicit apology for his own brutishness". We take it that they mean "apology" in the sense of justifying one's actions rather than in the sense of expressing guilt and expressing a desire to make amends for one's crimes. Because it acts as a justification, it is connected to Sade's crimes. At least intellectual works may also serve such a moral function. Martin Heidegger's work, for instance, has been claimed to have anti-Semitism at its core. Given this, Heidegger's work seems to take on the moral function of justifying his anti-Semitism. We might also make a similar case for other philosophical works, such as the work of Immanuel Kant. He expressed profoundly racist views in his work. We might wonder whether other aspects of his work serve to excuse or justify his racism.

When an achievement has such a moral function, we cannot in principle separate the achievement from the person's immorality. It is, in a sense, an extension of that immorality. While we may be able to separate other achievements from the person *in principle*, it does not follow that we can do so *in practice*. And it is often and perhaps typically much more important what you can and cannot do in practice. There are two factors we wish to highlight that affect the practical separation of achievement and person: public meaning and personal connection.

Consider first cases where the person is part of the achievement. Suppose that Cristiano Ronaldo is to be given an honour for his excellent goals just after having accepted a large fine for tax evasion. To give him an honour for his goals just after he has been convicted may justifiably seem to be condoning his crime, in part because it is given just as people have become aware of his wrongdoing. It could well be that those who give him the honour do condone his crime. However, our point is that even if they do not, it may still be reasonable for others to infer that they (the honourers) do condone his crime.

Something similar seems true in cases where there is only a responsibility link. Suppose we have a party to celebrate the film *Chinatown*. Polanski's film bears no obvious relation to his crime and is even critical of those who sexually harm children. Even so, *Chinatown* is Polanski's film. He is responsible for it (though of course many other people bear responsibility for it too, as filmmaking is a group endeavour). Because it is Polanski's film, by honouring and admiring that film – while it would not, strictly speaking, honour and admire him – there are many contexts in which it would reasonably appear to honour and admire him. Of course, we can say and do many things to avoid this public meaning. We can perhaps try to celebrate *Chinatown* while acknowledging that what Polanski did was wrong and so on. The point is not that we cannot honour and admire *Chinatown* without honouring and admiring Polanski. Rather, the point is that you sometimes have to do more than just focus on the achievement. When you *just* focus on Polanski's achievement, you may seem to be saying that you do not care about his crime, you do not care about his victim (Samantha Geimer), and you do not care about victims of similar crimes.

Finally, note the wider societal context in which honour and admiration currently take place. As we said in the previous section, there is currently a celebrity/hero culture that benefits and encourages us to globalize a person's achievements. While we think separating can help change this culture, this societal backdrop may often make such separation hard in practice.

There are also people who cannot practically separate because they bear some personal connection to the wrongs of the immoral person. Such people might either be victims of the immoral, relatives of victims of the immoral, or victims of similar crimes. It is understandable that such people might not be able to set aside their feelings and focus only on the achievement of such an immoral person.

We think it is plausible to understand this as a kind of volitional necessity, practical necessity, or moral incapacity, as discussed by philosophers such as Harry Frankfurt (1988) and Bernard Williams (1981, 1993).[6] The core of their respective ideas is that sometimes a person is simply unable to act in particular ways due to features of their character or past experiences.

While there are nuances to their respective views that we will not get into here, we think it is plausible to hold that the kind of resistance that some will have to honouring and admiring the immoral is like a volitional necessity. Because of their personal connection to the wrong, some people are not only psychologically unable to appreciate the excellence in a particular immoral person's achievement, but they also have an incapacity that is deeply expressive of their moral character. Of course, just because they have this incapacity, it does not mean that the person's achievement is not excellent.[7] While it is not only victims, relatives of victims, and victims of similar crimes who might have such an inability or resistance, it is most understandable in the case of such people. When such an incapacity is understandable, no one can expect those with such an incapacity to honour and admire achievements of particular immoral people. Importantly, those with such volitional necessities will be more prone – and perhaps justifiably so – to take an adverse public meaning from instances of honouring and admiring.

Even though you can focus on the achievement in many cases and this will not *necessarily* carry the moral dangers that can result from honouring and admiring the immoral, it often will have those moral dangers in practice – unless you take steps to avoid an adverse public meaning especially for those who have understandable volitional necessities against honouring and admiring the immoral. You cannot simply avoid moral dangers by pointing out that those dangers can be avoided in principle. You have to think about the moral dangers in any given context of honouring and admiring an immoral person. While the separating approach can sometimes be taken, it needs to be taken with great care.

4 The Ambiguity Approach

When it is not feasible to focus on the immoral person's achievements or on their admirable traits, you might still have sufficient reasons to admire them. Their work might be of such importance that you simply cannot ignore it. They might have made a great discovery in science and so you have to discuss their contribution in light of that achievement. And it might be that their immorality is tied up with their achievement or traits to such an extent that you cannot plausibly focus on only their achievement or traits without that at least having the public meaning of honouring and admiring their immoral traits and behaviour. As we argued in Chapter 2, this does not mean you would be honouring and admiring their immorality *in virtue of being* immoral, but their immorality might be honoured and admired nevertheless.

If you cannot honour and admire without some of this spreading over onto a person's immoral traits and immoral aspects of their achievements, then the final approach we will consider is that you simply accept that and use this as a kind of educational opportunity. In his discussion of Kant's racism, Victor Fabian Abundez-Guerra (2018) argues that there is reason to approach Kant's work with a stance of *deep acknowledgement*. He writes:

> What I mean by deep acknowledgment is a recognition of Kant's racial theory in a way that 1) it reflects on Kant's character, 2) Kant is held accountable for it and 3) one considers the possibility that it is not only consistent with, but also affects his traditional moral philosophy in significant ways so that one must revise their interpretation of Kant's moral theory.
>
> (Abundez-Guerra 2018: 126)

To properly understand Kant, then, we have to understand the racist element to his views and their relation to his otherwise egalitarian ethics. Deeply acknowledging Kant's work, according to Abundez-Guerra, involves examining whether Kant's racial views affect the rest of his philosophy, particularly his views on cosmopolitan rights, human dignity, and personhood. For example, Charles Mills (2017: Ch.6) takes this approach to Kant's philosophy and argues that Kant's views on rationality and personhood have to be understood alongside his views on irrationality and sub-personhood. According to Mills, this shows that Kant's moral philosophy cannot be separated from his views on race. Whether or not we agree with Mills' conclusion, the point Abundez-Guerra stresses is that we should be asking these kinds of questions when discussing Kant's work.

One option, then, is to approach certain artistic works with a stance of deep acknowledgement. As we discussed in Chapter 3, according to some critics there is an important connection between the ethical shortcomings of both Richard Wagner and Roman Polanski and the brilliance of their artistic creations. According to Lee (1999), Wagner's inner conflict allowed him to see more deeply into the troubling aspects of human nature. Similarly, Leaming (1982) claims that Polanski's films are important partly because of his amoral perspective. Given this, there is good reason to think that a true appreciation of the work requires a deep acknowledgement of their ethical shortcomings. We should not, then, seek to set the immorality of these artists to one side in appreciating their work. Rather, we should investigate the links between their ethical failings and their artistic achievements.

It might seem that this will be harder to achieve for public honours than the cases of private appreciation of someone's work considered so far. However, for cases of public honours we might seek to highlight this ambiguity through re-contextualizing these honours. Demetriou and Wingo (2018: 351) describe how in post-apartheid South Africa Nelson Mandela sought to steer his government away from completely destroying monuments that commemorate white colonizers: "the South African solution has been to remove the most offensive monuments of lesser importance, yes, but for the most part to add new monuments or reframe old ones". For example, a statue of Mandela was erected outside the Union Buildings in Pretoria, close to an old statue commemorating South Africa's first prime minister, Louis Botha. Similarly, the Voortrekker monument, a celebration of colonialization, has now been accompanied by a museum of Afrikaner culture and history that hires black tour guides and is connected to Freedom Park by Reconciliation Road. Demetriou and Wingo (2018: 351–352) argue that this approach provides a way of removing many of the harmful effects of these monuments without causing unnecessary social division which they claim will ultimately undermine antiracist goals. Rossi (2020: 76) also endorses this kind of approach, claiming that rather than remove statues of historically important but morally troubling figures, we should re-contextualize them in a way that no longer encourages unqualified admiration. While (as we discussed in Section 2) we are sceptical at minor efforts at re-contextualizing (such as a small plaque), we think that these more significant re-contextualization efforts are more promising.

While the focusing approach tries to use a person's immorality to ensure that focus remains on their admirable traits and achievements, the ambiguity approach emphasizes a person's immoral aspects. In both approaches, there is an implicit aim to emphasize a messy and complex – and indeed, more accurate – picture of a person. The focusing approach puts more emphasis on the admirable traits and achievements, whereas the ambiguity approach puts somewhat more emphasis on the immorality. However, both try to emphasize a more complete picture of a person. The reason for the difference in emphasis between these approaches is that the ambiguity approach most clearly becomes an appropriate option only when other options do not seem permissible. Doing nothing does not seem appropriate, but neither does abandoning admiration. Focusing – whether just on the work or on the person's admirable traits – does not seem to avoid the moral dangers of honouring and admiring. Because we cannot avoid honouring and admiring – perhaps for reasons of social cohesion, perhaps because the achievements are so important that they cannot be ignored, and so on – honouring and admiring the immoral then becomes an educational opportunity, an opportunity to expose ourselves to the dark sides of life, to realize that even wicked people can do things of excellence and great beauty.

Both the focusing approach and the ambiguity approach face the objection that they involve experiencing or expressing two conflicting emotions towards one person and that this is not possible. However, we think this is not only possible but quite common. Consider the mother whose love for her teenage daughter turns to anger when she stays out past her curfew. This is obvious insofar as one can be said to have an emotion when one is disposed to feeling in certain ways – for example, love and anger towards the same person when exposed to different stimuli. Yet one can also have conflicting feelings at the same time. While we have argued there may be a problem when we *prioritize* admiration over (say) indignation with respect to the admirable yet immoral, we are not always forced to make such a prioritization. We can instead express both simultaneously.

This might be thought to be a best-of-both-worlds approach. We can continue to honour and admire the admirable without promoting a wholly positive picture of them. In doing so, we respect both the reasons for and the reasons against honour and admiration. In particular, we may reduce the risk of othering wrongdoers and engaging in a misguided pursuit of purity. By continuing to celebrate the achievements of those who have acted immorally, we can send the message that these people remain members of the moral community, albeit members who have violated our moral norms.

Moreover, in comparison with the form of focused admiration considered above, this approach is one that may make more sense as a response to those whose admirable qualities and achievements cannot be separated from their immorality. This approach calls on people to attend to both these aspects of the person being admired and to consider the interrelations between the two. There is no need, then, to be able to separate the immoral from the admirable in order for this approach to work. While this approach offers a global assessment of the admired person, it is likely to be a more accurate global assessment. The admired qualities will be present alongside the flaws. It thus avoids the vice of globalism.

The ambiguous approach will often not be appropriate. It is most clearly appropriate when all other approaches seem impermissible and yet there are still strong reasons to honour and admire a particular achievement or person. However, there are many cases where the extent and the severity of the wrongdoing will make anything short of abandoning admiration inappropriate. For example, when revelations about Jimmy Savile's long history of sexual abuse emerged, a statue to Savile that had stood outside Scotstoun Leisure Centre in Glasgow was quickly removed. Charities with facilities named after Savile acted quickly to rename them. As someone who worked for one such charity points out, "There wasn't a single complaint" (McColl 2020). In cases like Savile's where someone's immoral behaviour erases anything else they may have done, re-contextualizing will not be desirable or effective. It is unreasonable to expect victims of child abuse to have to walk past a statue to Savile whenever they want to use their local swimming pool, no matter how this statue is re-contextualized.

While some statues might warrant being re-contextualized, we think that these will be exceptional cases – in particular, cases where re-contextualization is the best way to maintain social cohesion. Even important historical figures do not need a statue to be remembered. For example, statues commemorating figures like Edward Colston strike us as ones where re-contextualization is inappropriate. Colston was a major investor, manager, and deputy governor for the Royal African Company, a company that transported 84,500 enslaved Africans in conditions so unsanitary that 19,300 are estimated to have died in transit. Keeping statues of someone responsible for such horrific moral wrongs in prominent places is, in our view, completely inappropriate. While we could possibly re-contextualize his statues and his other public honours, it is not clear why this is necessary. Presenting a figure like Colston as an ambiguous figure who was admirable despite his involvement in the slave trade strikes us as an approach that significantly downplays the extent and significance of his actions, especially given that the things he may be admirable for – for example, his philanthropy, his courage, his daring – are hardly unique to him. If inspiration is needed for such things there are plenty of other people who could be honoured instead. Because it does not strike us as necessary with Colston, we think the ambiguous approach with respect to statues of him is inappropriate. Some readers may disagree with our assessment of this case. We hope that the general point is still clear.

While the ambiguity approach has a best-of-both-worlds feel to it, we think that it is not without its problems. For it to work, it must be clear that one is taking this approach. We think it may be easy for people to say that they are taking this approach – and say they are re-contextualizing something – but then not go to much effort to make this clear. The honour, then, might then still appear to be making a reductive global assessment of the person as purely admirable. There may also be those that focus too much on a person's wrongs. It may be that they are better served mentioning these wrongs and so drawing more attention to the person's admirable traits and achievements. As with the focusing and separating approaches, the ambiguity approach also faces problems with respect to our present celebrity/hero culture. Indeed, taking an ambiguous approach might also run the risk of glamourizing the immoral. As a result, when we have to honour and admire the immoral in this ambiguous way, we seem to be put into what Claudia Card (2002) calls a grey zone.[8] By this she means the further wrong of the immoral when they implicate us, to some extent, in their immorality. In other words, the ambiguous approach is not a morally clean option. We do unfortunately take on some of the taint of a person's immorality when we honour and admire them in this ambiguous way.

Again, let us emphasize that we think that the ambiguous approach is most obviously appropriate when all other approaches do not seem to be appropriate. It might be that after considering all the other approaches you find that abandoning admiration is the best option, after all. It might be, though, that the ambiguous approach is better in a particular case even though all the other options have not been exhausted. While we have presented the discussion so far as a kind of step-by-step guide, we do not want to convey that you have to match exactly this process. What is important, though, is to ask yourself the kinds of questions we have suggested throughout this book. This allows that there may be other relevant questions that we have missed. As we said in the Introduction, we hope to start a conversation by guiding people through an ethical puzzle that many of us encounter in daily life.

Notes

1 For more on the idea that we have mixed characters, see, for example, Miller (2014) and Hartman and Matheson (manuscript).

2 See also Smith (2021). Her research shows that people often overlook contextualizing information found on plaques added to controversial monuments. This supports our point that such plaques are fairly ineffective at contextualizing.

3 For more on these issues, see, for example, Matheson (2017a), Pettigrove (2004), and Radzik (2009).

4 Indeed, as Fabre (2016) argues, a problem with commemoration practices is that they are often partisan. This seems to make one side "the good guys" and the other side "the bad guys". In other words, it also seems to manifest the vice of globalism. Focusing on the good and bad actions of your own country during a war is one way that commemorative practices could avoid this, and so it is one way to morally improve commemorative practices.

5 The worry is distinct from that found in the longstanding debate about immoral art. It may be well that we have independent reason not to honour and admire an immoral artwork *because* it is less aesthetically valuable due to some of its features – for example, the artwork endorses immoral attitudes (e.g. Carroll 1996; Gaut 2007; Bartel 2019). See Chapter 2 for discussion. Our current concern is rather whether we have reason not to honour and admire achievements (including artworks) because they have a bad moral function.

6 See also Archer (2015) and Matheson (2017b).

7 There is a connection here with discussions of *imaginative resistance* (e.g. Gendler 2000). This is the idea that certain features of artworks or narratives are jarring such that we cannot or will not fully imagine them – for example, we cannot imagine that certain moral truths are false. Some, such as Eva Dadlez (2005), argue that features of immoral artworks give rise to imaginative resistance and that this decreases the aesthetic value of the work. Others, such as Jacobson (1997), hold that imaginative resistance blocks us from seeing the value rather than undermining its values and, thus, is a problem with the viewer of the art rather than the artwork. One way to understand what is happening in these cases is that there is a kind of moral incapacity: not only can we not act in particular ways, sometimes we cannot even imagine in particular ways.

8 Card takes this term from Primo Levi (1988: Ch.2)

Conclusion

How should you respond to an immoral yet admirable person? Should you honour and admire such a person? Should you instead blame and shun them? Throughout this book we have outlined a number of factors that affect what decision you should make. We have not given a precise formula for working out the best response, as we have aimed to provide a guide to thinking about the ethical puzzle of how we should treat immoral yet admirable people. However, we do recommend asking the following general questions.

1 Is the Person Really a Fitting Target of Admiration?

You should first establish that you are dealing with an instance of the puzzle. This requires that you have a person who is a fitting target of admiration *and* who is immoral. As we argued in Chapter 1, to be a fitting target of admiration a person must be, or have achieved, something extraordinarily excellent. As we explained in Chapter 2, there are at least three ways someone's immoral behaviour may prevent them from being a fitting target of admiration. First, it may serve as an epistemic defeater, one that undermines the reasons people have for thinking that the person acted in ways that are worthy of admiration. As the case of Jimmy Savile illustrated, someone may appear to have acted admirably (at least to some people), when in fact these acts were all performed in order to facilitate appalling acts of abuse. Second, it might be that their immorality affects the value of their work. For example, learning about Marquis de Sade's real-life immorality might make you think that his work is not as excellent as you previously thought. Third, a person's immoral behaviour may prevent that person from remaining admirable for some earlier action. For example, Aung San Suu Kyi may no longer be a fitting target of admiration for the acts that led to her receiving the Nobel Peace Prize after her failure to speak

DOI: 10.4324/9780367810153

out against the war crimes committed by her country's military. If it turns out that a person is a not a fitting target of admiration (for any reason), you have an easy answer: you should not honour and admire this person.

But sometimes a person is both admirable and immoral. We think this is true of Roman Polanski. He remains a fitting target of admiration for his aesthetic talents and achievements despite having committed a horrific act of sexual assault on a child. While you might disagree about the example, we take it that there are many cases where someone is a fitting target of admiration despite their immoral behaviour. In cases like this, the fact that someone is a fitting target of admiration provides some reason to admire them. But this is merely the start of the deliberative process, as the fact that someone is a fitting target of admiration provides, at most, a defeasible reason to admire that person.

Importantly, you might start this deliberative process even in cases where we are not completely certain a person is either admirable or immoral. You might have good evidence that someone has acted immorally and yet not be completely certain about this. You might have good evidence and be open to being proven wrong. You will often have to make a decision about whether you will honour and admire a person without having certainty. You will not often have the liberty to wait until all the facts come and are indisputable before deciding what to do. This is one factor that makes real ethical decision-making difficult. Sometimes you will have to decide on the basis of your evidence, and sometimes you will get it wrong. The harms related to being wrong about the facts will have to be weighed against the moral dangers of honouring and admiring or refraining from honouring and admiring.

2   Are There Moral Reasons That Count against Honour and Admiration in This Case?

First, you should ask whether your honour or admiration might empower the wrongdoer. If there is a risk that it will be interpreted as condoning the immoral behaviour, picking the wrongdoer out as an exemplar, enhancing their credibility, or providing them with normative support, then it may empower them. If so, then there is reason not to honour and admire them.

Second, you must ask whether the honouring and admiring of the wrongdoer risks harming the wrongdoer's victims. In answering this question, we must ask whether in honouring and admiring a wrongdoer you may be disrespecting their victims. One important way to investigate this issue is to consider what victims themselves say about whether it would be disrespectful to honour and admire their wrongdoer. Of course, this may not generate any clear answers, as victims may disagree on this issue. Even where they agree, that is no guarantee that they are right to feel that honouring and admiring their wrongdoer would disrespect them. Nevertheless, this seems like a worthwhile place to start, both because victims are likely to have important insights on this issue and because the act of listening to victims is itself a clear way to show that they are respected. Even if you are not contributing to harm yourself, you must also ask whether in honouring and admiring a wrongdoer you are making yourself complicit in their wrongdoing. You must also ask if there is a risk that honouring and admiring a wrongdoer would silence their victims. An important question to consider here is whether those victims are in danger of being ignored. For instance, public discussions of the wrongdoing may focus entirely on the wrongdoer's side of the story. The wrongdoer may be an especially powerful person who is capable of mobilizing significant support for their side of the story. The victim may be a member of a marginalized group and so especially vulnerable to being ignored. In addition, the wrongdoing in question may be the kind of wrong in which victims' stories are systematically downplayed or ignored, such as with rape and domestic violence.

Third, you must ask if through honouring and admiring the wrongdoer, you are perpetuating wrongdoing, either by encouraging others to emulate the wrongdoer or by supporting a harmful ideology. This reason will not be present in all cases. There will sometimes be little danger of the honour and admiration being interpreted in a way that would present someone as an exemplar. Moreover, in some cases honouring and admiring a wrongdoer will not support any harmful ideologies.

If none of these reasons against honour and admiration are present, then we may have a simple solution to the question of what to do. In this case, we may be able to honour and admire without any problems at all, though of course there may also be other reasons not to do so that we have not considered. If one or more of these reasons are present, then we should consider the next question.

3 Are There Reasons That Count in Favour of Honour and Admiration?

The first question to ask here is whether in addition to being a fitting target of admiration, the person also *deserves* to be admired. Those who create great artworks, make ground-breaking contributions to intellectual life, or shape a society's history in positive ways generally deserve to be honoured and admired. There are stronger reasons to give people what they deserve than to give them what is fitting. Even so, as we emphasized in Chapter 3, the reasons that desert gives are still defeasible. There may be reasons against honouring and admiring someone who deserves admiration that mean that, all-things-considered, we should not admire them.

Moreover, the fact that someone deserves honour and admiration does not mean that it is any particular individual's responsibility to ensure that they receive this. Those with no interest in cinema may have little or no reason to ensure that Polanski is admired for his talents as a filmmaker. Similarly, those left cold by opera have little reason to ensure that Wagner is honoured and admired. On the other hand, an awards committee deciding who should receive the best director award have a far greater responsibility to ensure that filmmakers receive the honour and admiration they deserve. In addition to asking yourself whether someone deserves honour and admiration, you should also consider whether you have any responsibility to ensure that they get what they deserve. If it is your responsibility to ensure someone gets the honour and admiration they deserve, then you will have a much stronger reason to honour and admire them.

In addition to asking whether someone deserves an honour or admiration, you should also ask whether they are entitled to it. Even if they are only entitled to an honour, they may be entitled to forms of honour that encourage admiration, such as a prize, a medal, or some other form of award. If an award has clear and precise criteria governing who should receive it then the person who meets these criteria is likely to be entitled to the award. A clear case of this is a 100-metre sprint race: the winner is the person who crosses the finish line first without breaking any of the relevant rules and they seem entitled to the prize, which means that they have a right to it. An entitlement claim, then, generally provides a stronger reason to ensure someone receives an honour than a desert claim, though even these claims might be overridden in exceptional circumstances. As with desert, so with entitlement: it does not follow that you or any particular person has a duty to admire or honour.

The next question to ask when seeking to identify which reasons are in play concerns the issue of moralism. As we argued in Chapter 3, the most relevant charge of moralism in this context is that a moralistic approach leads to people closing themselves off from valuable experiences. When considering a particular case of honouring or admiring someone who has acted immorally, you should consider whether you may be operating with an inflated sense of the appropriateness of moral criticism and are losing out on valuable experiences as a result. This is unlikely to be an easy question to answer, as there is no simple way to determine whether one is giving too much weight to moral concerns. Indeed, you must be careful not to manifest the opposing vice of moral indifference. Nevertheless, it is important to bear in mind that moral reasons are not the only reasons to consider when deciding how to respond to any particular case. You should also consider the aesthetic and epistemic reasons you may have to admire great artists, intellectuals, and historical figures. In considering any particular case, you should ask whether their works and achievements are truly exceptional. More generally, you should ask whether in refusing to admire those who have acted immorally you might be shutting yourself off from distinctive contributions and insights into the human condition. Finally, you should consider whether someone's achievements have played an important role in shaping your identity. If so, then this might justify continuing to honour and admire that person even when there are good moral reasons that count against doing so. Of course, sometimes you will have to accept the damage to your identity and cease honouring and admiring someone.

If none of these considerations seem relevant, then it may be clear how you should act. If there are forceful reasons against honour and admiration and nothing counting in its favour, then abandoning honour and admiration is likely to be the best response. However, things will often be more complicated, and you will face a range of reasons counting both in favour of and against honour and admiration. Here, you should consider whether one of these sets of reasons is clearly more forceful than the other set, including considering the strength of evidence in favour of these reasons. If there is still not a clear winner, then you should consider the following question.

4 Would a Focused Form of Honour and Admiration Be the Best Approach?

The first focused approach is to ensure that honour and admiration does not spread beyond a person's admirable traits and achievements. This approach has the advantage of allowing these admirable qualities to be celebrated while avoiding or at least reducing the moral problems that may arise from doing so. Importantly, it helps to avoid an overly simplistic view of people as merely good or bad that we argued arises from the vice of globalism, which involves globalizing a feature of a person so that it comes to be seen as the entirety of who they are.

The second focused approach instead concentrates only on the achievements of an immoral person. This approach separates the achievements from the person. Again, this approach may offer a way to celebrate the admirable achievements without celebrating the person. However, this may also be difficult to achieve when someone's work and achievements are difficult to separate from their immorality. Care should be taken that this focused form of honour and admiration will be understood to be only about a person's admirable traits and achievements and as a global endorsement of the person.

Finally, we might seek to honour and admire someone in a way that recognizes and engages with their immorality – what we called the ambiguity approach. This approach is particularly well suited for cases where someone's admirable qualities and achievements cannot be separated from their immorality. It also seems to be a way of responding to someone's ethical failings without othering that person or engaging in a misguided purity project. Moreover, it allows us to investigate the links between their achievements and their ethical failings. However, this response may not be appropriate in all cases. There are cases where someone's wrongdoings are too severe to make ambiguous representations appropriate. It is most appropriate when all other approaches seem inappropriate and yet you find you still need to honour and admire a person in some way. There are also cases where the wrongdoings are too minor to justify an ambiguous response.

One of the last three approaches may be the most appropriate response when a person has been accused of immorality but it is not clear whether the accusations are true. Each of these approaches, after all, aims to promote a broader, more complicated understanding of who people are. This complicated understanding might include the fact that we do not know everything about them and that there are questions that remain about whether they have done something immoral. Such an understanding may be supported by a tentative act of blame or protest at the wrongdoer which could draw attention to the accusation of serious wrongdoing. For example, when Casey Affleck was awarded the Oscar for Best Actor in 2017, Brie Larson, the award's presenter, refused to applaud him. Speaking after the ceremony, Larson, a vocal advocate for victims of sexual assault, said her behaviour "Spoke for itself" (Chi 2017).

By refusing to applaud Affleck, Larson expressed a soft condemnation of Affleck to accompany the admiration being expressed and encouraged by the award. We are thereby given a picture of him as someone who is not just admirable but also someone who might have acted wrongly.

Not only must you consider the strength of the evidence that you have for a person's immorality and admirability and the strength of those reasons, but you must also consider how other people are reacting to the person. As we discussed, the appropriateness of actions and feelings can be affected by what others are doing. If everyone is blaming a particular person, you might have no need to. Indeed, you might have good reason not to. Each person's blame, taken together, may be disproportionate and thus a manifestation of moralism. Likewise, if many people are honouring and admiring a particular person, then you might have no need to. Everyone's honour and admiration, taken together, might manifest the vice of moral indifference. If others are not honouring and admiring in appropriate ways, you might, however, have good reason to step in and set an example about a more appropriate way to honour and admire – such as ensuring that honour and admiration is focused and does not spread over onto their immoral traits and actions.

***

While we have offered a number of questions that might be asked to try and determine how to respond to a particular case, we offer no general formula for deciding which reasons we should prioritize in any particular case. This may seem disappointing to those looking for clear guidance about how to act. However, we believe that any attempt to provide such a formula is misguided. Moral conflicts often involve difficult decisions calling for fine-grained, contextual judgements which we should not seek to solve through discovering a general, systematic formula. As Aristotle (350 B.C.E [2009] Bk. 1 Ch.3) points out, a discussion should only be as precise as its subject matter allows: we believe that the field of ethics does not allow for the precision of a systematic formula. Moreover, as Sophie Grace Chappell (2014: Ch.1) points out, the absence of any systematic formulae for ethical decision-making does not mean that there is no such thing as a good ethical decision.

The absence of a simple manual means that having answered each of the above questions we must then reflect carefully on whether honour and admiration are appropriate in this case.

These decisions will not be easy, and there are likely to be cases where whatever we decide will involve acting against important reasons that count against this course of action.

There may even be more than one option that is morally permissible. There may be cases where the reasons counting in favour and against honour and admiration are of roughly equal strength and so neither option is better than the other. Perhaps more likely, there may be cases where one of these options is preferable from the moral point of view but is not morally required. It is widely accepted that some acts are beyond the call of duty (i.e. supererogatory).[1] These are acts that are morally better than some other permissible form of action but that are not morally required. Risking one's own life to save that of another, for example, will often be morally better than making no effort to save that person's life but will often not be required. However, supererogatory acts need not be so extreme. Helping a neighbour home with their shopping may also be good, but doing so may go beyond any duty you owe to your neighbour. What this shows is that even if we have identified the act that would be morally best, we may still face the question of whether it is morally required. Perhaps the personal sacrifice involved in abandoning our admiration would be so great that we are not required to make it, even though it would be the morally preferable option.[2]

We have focused on how individuals or organizations may respond to these issues. It is important to note that one of the main barriers to the focused forms of admiration discussed in Chapter 5 is a celebrity culture that treats great artists, sports people, intellectuals, scientists, and politicians as heroes to be worshipped. This encourages global admiration of those who are honoured and admired, as well as encouraging us to overlook other people who have been involved in bringing about the achievements of people who are honoured and admired. It is important for individuals to take this culture into account when deciding whether to honour and admire the immoral, as it will influence how their honouring and admiration is interpreted by others.

We think that the culture that seeks to turn people into celebrities is open to challenge. We see this book as one small step towards challenging this culture. If in future we generally honour and admire people in focused ways, we may avoid manifesting or encouraging the vice of globalism, which we think is a key part of this culture. There are, though, many more critical questions to be investigated as part of this process. How should people respond when others choose to honour and admire those who in their view should not be honoured and admired? How should we assess the responsibilities of fans in sustaining celebrity culture? What responsibility do celebrities themselves have to challenge this culture? While some of these questions have been investigated by those working in celebrity studies, we think it is important for philosophers to start to take these questions seriously too.[3]

What is called for here is not just more philosophical attention to these issues but a wider societal challenge to celebrity culture. The history of the American film industry shows the contingent nature of celebrity culture. At the beginning of the twentieth century, The Edison Trust had a monopoly of the industry and sought to prevent actors from acquiring celebrity status by prohibiting artistic credits and refusing licences for films featuring star-making performances. They were largely successful in doing so until a group of independent filmmakers started a rival film industry in Hollywood, which was more open turning actors into stars (Wu 2010: 61–73). So, celebrity culture is not inevitable. Indeed, people sustain celebrity culture by paying attention to celebrities (van Krieken 2012: 73). If this attention were withdrawn, then this culture would be very difficult to sustain. Given a widespread collective effort, then, it would be possible to challenge this celebrity culture.

While any individual's ability to influence this culture is likely to be limited, it will also be impossible to change this culture unless there are individual efforts to resist it. You should seek to avoid encouraging and manifesting the vice of globalism by recognizing that great talents may exist alongside deep moral flaws. By taking such a stance towards those you admire, you can play some small part in resisting the damaging tendency to think of people in simplistic and reductive ways. People's flaws need not define who they are but nor should these flaws be ignored, downplayed, justified, or excused simply because of someone's talents and achievements.

Notes

1 However, some deny their existence. For a summary of this debate, see Archer (2018b).
2 Many hold that the level of sacrifice involved is always what prevents an act of supererogation from being obligatory (e.g. Benn 2018). Even those who deny this (e.g. Archer 2015, 2016) accept that the level of sacrifice is *often* what prevents the morally best act from being obligatory.
3 Philosophers have already begun to explore this issue in relation to statues commemorating those implicated in racism and slavery – see Lim (2020) and Ten-Herng Lai (2020) – but these questions have not been explored in relation to other cases of admiring the immoral.

Bibliography

Abrahams, D.A. (forthcoming). "The Importance of History to the Erasing-history Defence". *Journal of Applied Philosophy.*

Abundez-Guerra, V.F. (2018). "How to Deal with Kant's Racism – In and out of the Classroom". *Teaching Philosophy.* doi:10.5840/teachphil201851185.

Adam, K. (2015). "U.K. Marks the 50th Anniversary of Winston Churchill's Funeral – And What a Funeral It Was". *The Washington Post.* https://www.washingtonpost.com/news/worldviews/wp/2015/01/30/u-k-marks-the-50th-anniversary-of-winston-churchills-funeral-and-what-a-funeral-it-was/ [Accessed: 19/04/2021]

Algoe, S.B., and Haidt, J. (2009). "Witnessing Excellence in Action: The 'Other-Praising' Emotions of Elevation, Gratitude, and Admiration". *The Journal of Positive Psychology* 4 (2):105–127.

Appiah, K.A. (2018). *The Lies That Bind: Rethinking Identity.* Liveright Publishing Corporation.

Aquino, K., McFerran, B., and Laven, M. (2011). "Moral Identity and the Experience of Moral Elevation in Response to Acts of Uncommon Goodness". *Journal of Personality and Social Psychology* 100 (4):703–718.

Aratani, L., and Pilkington, Ed. (2020). "Harvey Weinstein Sentenced to 23 Years in Prison on Rape Conviction". *The Guardian.* https://www.theguardian.com/world/2020/mar/11/harvey-weinstein-sentencing-rape-conviction [Accessed: 19/04/2021].

Archer, A. (2014). "Moral Rationalism without Overridingness". *Ratio* 27 (1):100–114.

Archer, A. (2015). "Saints, Heroes and Moral Necessity". *Royal Institute of Philosophy Supplement* 77:105–124.

Archer, A. (2016). "Supererogation, Sacrifice, and the Limits of Duty". *Southern Journal of Philosophy* 54 (3):333–354.

Archer, A. (2018a). "The Problem with Moralism". *Ratio* 31 (3):342–350.

Archer, A. (2018b). "Supererogation". *Philosophical Compass* 13 (3).

Archer, A. (2019). "Admiration and Motivation". *Emotion Review* 11 (2):140–150.

Archer, A., Cawston, A., Matheson, B., and Geuskens, M. (2020). "Celebrity, Democracy and Epistemic Power". *Perspectives on Politics* 18 (1):27–42.

Archer, A., and Matheson, B. (2019a). "When Artists Fall: Honoring and Admiring the Immoral". *Journal of the American Philosophical Association* 5 (2):246–265.

Archer, A., and Matheson, B. (2019b). "Admiration and Education: What Should We Do with Immoral Intellectuals?" *Ethical Perspectives* 26 (1):5–32.

Archer, A., and Matheson, B. (2019c). "Shame and the Sports Fan". *Journal of the Philosophy of Sport* 46 (2):208–223.

Archer, A., and Matheson, B. (2020). "Admiration over Time". *Pacific Philosophical Quarterly* 101 (4):669–689.

Archer, A., and Mills, G. (2019). "Anger, Affective Injustice and Emotion Regulation". *Philosophical Topics*. 46 (2):75–94.

Aristotle (2009 [350 B.C.E.]). *The Nicomachean Ethics*. Translated by W.D. Ross. Oxford University Press.

Arnold, N.S. (1987). "Why Profits Are Deserved". *Ethics* 97 (2):387–402.

Attar, S. (2010). *Debunking the Myths of Colonization: The Arabs and Europe*. University Press of America.

BAFTA (2019). "A Statement Regarding Bryan Singer and His Film Awards Nomination". http://www.bafta.org/media-centre/press-releases/statement-6-feb-2019. [Accessed: 07/02/2019].

Bahiana, A.M. (2017). "Oprah Winfrey: Recipient of the Cecil B. DeMille Award 2018". *Golden Globe Awards*. https://www.goldenglobes.com/articles/oprah-winfrey-recipient-cecil-b-demille-award-2018 [Accessed: 19/04/2021]

Baron, M. (1986). "On Admirable Immorality". *Ethics* 96.

Bartel, C. (2019). "Ordinary Monsters: Ethical Criticism and the Lives of Artists". *Contemporary Aesthetics* 17:18.

Barthes, R. (1967/1977). "The Death of the Author". *Image, Music, Text*. Translated by S. Heath. Hill and Wang: 142–148.

BBC News (2002). "Churchill Voted Greatest Briton". (24/11/2002). http://news.bbc.co.uk/2/hi/entertainment/2509465.stm [Accessed: 19/04/2021]

Bedworth, C. (2018). "Paul Gauguin – Master or Monster?" *Daily Art Magazine*. https://www.dailyartmagazine.com/gauguin-master-or-monster/ [Accessed: 19/04/2021]

Begley, S. (2019). "The Surgeon Had a Dilemma Only a Nazi Medical Text Could Resolve. Was It Ethical to Use It?" *Stat*. (30/5/2019). https://www.statnews.com/2019/05/30/surgical-dilemma-only-nazi-medical-text-could-resolve/ [Accessed: 18/12/2020].

Bell, M. (2011). "Globalist Attitudes and the Fittingness Objection". *Philosophical Quarterly* 61 (244):449–472.

Benn, C. (2018). "Supererogation, Optionality and Cost". *Philosophical Studies* 176:2399–2417.

Ben-Ze'ev, A. (2000). *The Subtlety of Emotions*. MIT Press.

Berninger, A. (forthcoming). "Commemorating Public Figures – In Favour of a Fictionalist Position". *Journal of Applied Philosophy*.

Bhattacharjee, A., Berman, J.Z., and Reed, A. (2013). "Tip of the Hat, Wag of the Finger: How Moral Decoupling Enables Consumers to Admire and Admonish". *Journal of Consumer Research* 39 (6):1167–1184.

Binnie, I. (2019). "Soccer Star Ronaldo to Answer Tax Fraud Charges in Spain". *Reuters* (21/1/2019). https://www.reuters.com/article/uk-soccer-taxation-ronaldo/soccer-star-ronaldo-to-answer-tax-fraud-charges-in-spain-idUKKCN1PF1O0?edition-redirect=uk [Accessed: 19/04/2021]

Boorstin, D. (1961). *The Image: A Guide to Pseudo-Events in America*. New York: Atheneum.

Bradley, L. (2019). "Roman Polanski Compares His Rape Case to the Dreyfus Affair in New Interview". *Vanity Fair.* (29/8/2019). https://www.vanityfair.com/hollywood/2019/08/roman-polanski-an-officer-and-a-spy-rape-allegations-interview [Accessed: 5/1/2021].

Brady, E. (2013). *The Sublime in Modern Philosophy: Aesthetics, Ethics, and Nature*. Cambridge University Press.

Brown Harris, F. (1965). "Standing Securely on Both Feet" cited in Staltonstall. Leverett "Winston Churchill" *Congressional Record: Proceedings and Debates of the 89th Congress – First Session*, Volume III – Part 2, January 28 1965 – February 16 1965.

Burch-Brown, J. (2017). "Is It Wrong to Topple Statues and Rename Schools". *Journal of Political Theory and Philosophy* 1:59–86.

Burch-Brown, J. (forthcoming). "Should Slavery's Statues Be Preserved? On Transitional Justice and Contested Heritage". *Journal of Applied Philosophy*.

Burke, E. (1999 [1790]). *Reflections on the Revolution in France*. Oxford University Press.

Burrowes, N. (2013). "Responding to the Challenge of Rape Myths in Court (London: NB Research)". http://www.nb-research.com/wp-content/uploads/2015/01/Responding-to-the-challenge-of-rape-myths-in-court_Nina-Burrowes.pdf [Accessed 19/04/2021]

Burt, M.R. (1980). "Cultural Myths and Supports for Rape". *Journal of Personality and Social Psychology* 38 (2):217–230.

Card, C. (2002). *The Atrocity Paradigm: A Theory of Evil*. Oxford University Press.

Carlsson, A. (2017). "Blameworthiness as Deserved Guilt". *The Journal of Ethics* 21 (1):89–115.

Carroll, N. (1996). "Moderate Moralism". *The British Journal of Aesthetics* 36 (3):223–239.

Cawston, A. (2019). "Admiring Animals". In A. Archer and A. Grahlé (eds), *The Moral Psychology of Admiration* (pp. 165–178). Rowman and Littlefield.

Chappell, S.G. (2014). *Knowing What to Do: Imagination, Virtue, and Platonism in Ethics* Oxford University Press.

Chappell, S.G. (2019). "No More Heroes Any More?" In A. Archer and A. Grahlé (eds), *The Moral Psychology of Admiration* (pp. 11–28). Rowman and Littlefield.

Chi, P. (2017). "Brie Larson Says Not Clapping for Casey Affleck at the Oscars 'Speaks for Itself'". *Vanity Fair.* https://www.vanityfair.com/hollywood/2017/03/brie-larson-casey-affleck-not-clapping-oscars-best-actor [Accessed: 01/12/2017].

C.K., L. (2017). "Louis C.K. Responds to Accusations: 'These Stories Are True'". *The New York Times*. https://www.nytimes.com/2017/11/10/arts/television/louis-ck-statement.html?auth=login-email&login=email [Accessed: 19/04/2021].

Coady, C.A.J. (2008). *Messy Morality: The Challenge of Politics*. Oxford University Press.

Cohen, G.A. (2013). *Finding Oneself in the Other*. Princeton University Press.

Coscarelli, J. (2019). "Michael Jackson Fans Are Tenacious. 'Leaving Neverland' Has Them Poised for Battle". *The New York Times*. https://www.nytimes.com/2019/03/04/arts/music/michael-jackson-leaving-neverland-fans.html [Accessed: 19/04/2021]

Costanzo, M.A., and Gerrity, E. (2009). "The Effects and Effectiveness of Using Torture as an Interrogation Device: Using Research to Inform the Policy Debate". *Social Issues and Policy Review* 3 (1):179–210.

Cox, K.S. (2010). "Elevation Predicts Domain-Specific Volunteerism 3 Months Later". *The Journal of Positive Psychology* 5 (5):333–341.

Cummiskey, D. (1987). "Desert and Entitlement: A Rawlsian Consequentialist Account". *Analysis* 47 (1):15–19.

Curry, T. (2017). *The Man-Not: Race, Class, Genre, and the Dilemmas of Black Manhood*. Temple University Press.

Curzer, H.J. (2002). "Admirable Immorality, Dirty Hands, Care Ethics, Justice Ethics, and Child Sacrifice". *Ratio* 15 (3):227–244.

D'Arms, J., and Jacobson, D. (2000). "The Moralistic Fallacy: On the 'Appropriateness' of Emotions". *Philosophy and Phenomenological Research* 61 (1):65–90.

D'Arms, J., and Jacobson, D. (2003). "The Significance of Recalcitrant Emotion (or, Anti-quasijudgmentalism)". *Royal Institute of Philosophy Supplement* 52:127–145.

Dadlez, E.M. (2005). "Knowing Setter: The Epistemic Underpinnings of Moral Criticism of Fiction". *Southwest Philosophy Review* 21 (1):35–44.

Darwall, S. (1977). "Two Kinds of Respect". *Ethics* 88 (1):36–49.

Darwin, C. (1872/1998). *The Expression of the Emotions in Man and Animals*. Oxford University Press.

Demetriou, D., and Wingo, A. (2018). "The Ethics of Racist Monuments". In D. Boonin (ed.), *Palgrave Handbook of Philosophy and Public Policy* (pp. 341–355). Palgrave.

Deonna, J.A., Rodogno, R., and Teroni, F. (2012). *In Defense of Shame: The Faces of an Emotion*. Oxford University Press.

Deonna, J.A., and Teroni, F. (2015). "Emotions as Attitudes". *Dialectica* 69 (3):293–311.

Deuchert, E., Adjamah, K., and Pauly, F. (2005). "For Oscar Glory or Oscar Money?" *Journal of Cultural Economics* 29 (3):159–176.

Donvan, J.J., and Zucker, C.B. (2016). *In a Different Key: The Story of Autism*. Crown Publishing.

Doris, J.M. (2003). *Lack of Character: Personality and Moral Behavior*. Cambridge University Press.

Dotson, K. (2011). "Tracking Epistemic Violence, Tracking Practices of Silencing". *Hypatia* 26 (2): 236–257.

Douglas, M. (1966). *Purity and Danger: An Analysis of Concepts of Pollution and Taboo*. Routledge.

Driver, J. (2006). "Moralism". In C.A.J. Coady (ed.), *What's Wrong with Moralism*. Blackwell: 37–52.

Dunn, S. (1994). *New and Selected Poems, 1974–1994*. W. W. Norton.

Elicker, B. (2021). "Why We Should Avoid Artists Who Cause Harm: Support as Enabling Harm". *Journal of Applied Philosophy* 38 (2): 306–319.

Fabre, C. (2016). *Cosmopolitan Peace*. Oxford University Press.

Feinberg, J. (1970). "Justice and Personal Desert". In M. Friedman, L. May, K. Parsons, and J. Stiff (eds), *Rights and Reason: Essays in Honor of Carl Wellman* (pp. 221–250). Springer.

Feldman, F., and Skow, B. "Desert". In E.N. Zalta (ed.), *The Stanford Encyclopedia of Philosophy* (Winter 2019 Edition). https://plato.stanford. edu/archives/win2019/entries/desert/

Flaherty, C. (2018). "Harassment and Power". *Inside HigherEd* (28/8/2018). https://www.insidehighered.com/news/2018/08/20/some-say-particulars-ronell-harassment-case-are-moot-it-all-comes-down-power [Accessed: 19/04/2021].

Forrester, M.G. (1982). *Moral Language*. University of Wisconsin Press.

Frankfurt, H.G. (1988). *The Importance of What We Care about: Philosophical Essays*. Cambridge University Press.

Freeman, D., Aquino, K., and McFerran, B. (2009). "Overcoming Beneficiary Race as an Impediment to Charitable Donations: Social Dominance Orientation, the Experience of Moral Elevation, and Donation Behavior". *Personality and Social Psychology Bulletin* 35 (1):72–84.

Fricker, M. (2007). *Epistemic Injustice: The Power and Ethics of Knowing*. Oxford University Press.

Fullinwider, R.K. (2006). "On Moralism". In C.A.J. Coady (ed.), *What's Wrong with Moralism* (pp. 5–20). Blackwell.

Gaut, B. (2007). *Art, Emotion and Ethics*. Oxford University Press.

Gendler, T.S. (2000). "The Puzzle of Imaginative Resistance". *Journal of Philosophy* 97 (2):55–81.

Geuskens, M. (2018). *Epistemic Justice: A Principled Approach to Knowledge Generation and Distribution*. PhD dissertation, Tilburg University, Tilburg, The Netherlands. Retrieved from Tilburg University Research Portal: https://pure.uvt.nl/ws/portalfiles/portal/28669897/Geuskens_ Epistemic_11_12_2018.pdf. [Accessed 21/4/2021].

Gilbert, M. (2002). "Collective Guilt and Collective Guilt Feelings". *The Journal of Ethics* 6 (2):115–143.

Golub, C. (2019). "Personal Value, Biographical Identity, and Retrospective Attitudes". *Australasian Journal of Philosophy* 97 (1):72–85.

Grady, C. (2019). "What Do We Do When the Art We Love Was Created by a Monster?" *Vox*. https://www.vox.com/culture/2018/10/11/17933686/

me-too-separating-artist-art-johnny-depp-woody-allen-michael-jackson-louis-ck [Accessed: 19/04/2021]

Gräf, M., and Unkelbach, C. (2016). "Halo Effects in Trait Assessment Depend on Information Valence: Why Being Honest Makes You Industrious, but Lying Does Not Make You Lazy". *Personality and Social Psychology Bulletin* 42:290–310.

Grahle, A. (2019). "Admiration as Normative Support". In A. Archer and A. Grahlé (eds), *The Moral Psychology of Admiration* (pp. 149–164). Rowman and Littlefield.

Greer, R. (2019, January 25). "Once Again for the People in the Back: Churchill Was a White Supremacist Mass Murderer". [Twitter Post]. https://twitter.com/Ross_Greer/status/1088871720382091264 [Accessed: 17/10/2019].

Grice, H.P. (1957). "Meaning". *Philosophical Review* 66 (3):377–388.

Gross, J.J. (2015). "Emotion Regulation: Current Status and Future Prospects". *Psychological Inquiry* 26 (1):1–26.

Guinn, J. (2009). *Go Down Together: The True, Untold Story of Bonnie and Clyde*. Simon & Schuster.

Hall, S. (1996). "The Problem of Ideology: Marxism without Guarantees". In D. Morlay and K.-H. Chen (eds), *(Un)Settling Accounts: Marxism & Cultural Studies* (pp. 25–46). Routledge.

Hartman, R., and Matheson, B. (manuscript). "The out of Character Objection to the Character Condition on Moral Responsibility".

Haslanger, S. (2012). *Resisting Reality: Social Construction and Social Critique*. Oxford University Press.

Haslanger, S. (2017a). "I – Culture and Critique". *Aristotelian Society Supplementary Volume* 91 (1):149–173.

Haslanger, S. (2017b). "Racism, Ideology, and Social Movements". *Res Philosophica* 94 (1):1–22.

Henley, J. (2017). "Calls to Boycott French Film Awards over Roman Polanski Honor". *The Guardian*. (20/1/2017). https://www.theguardian.com/film/2017/jan/20/womens-groups-boycott-cesar-french-film-awards-roman-polanski [Accessed: 24/10/2017].

Hennekam, S., and Bennett, D. (2017). "Sexual Harassment in the Creative Industries: Tolerance, Culture and the Need for Change". *Gender, Work & Organization*. 24(3): 417–434.

Hill, A. (2001). "Gauguin's Erotic Tahiti Idyll Exposed as a Sham". *The Guardian*. https://www.theguardian.com/world/2001/oct/07/arts.highereducation [Accessed: 19/04/2021]

Howard, C. (2018). "Fittingness". *Philosophy Compass* 13 (11).

Hughes, P.M., and Warmke, B. (2017). "Forgiveness". In E. Zalta (ed.), *The Stanford Encyclopedia of Philosophy*. https://plato.stanford.edu/archives/sum2017/entries/forgiveness/

Immordino-Yang, M.H., and Sylvan, L. (2010). "Admiration for Virtue: Neuroscientific Perspectives on a Motivating Emotion". *Contemporary Educational Psychology* 35 (2):110–115.

Jacobson, D. (1997). "In Praise of Immoral Art". *Philosophical Topics* 25 (1):155–199.

Jauss, S. (2008). "Review: What's Wrong with Moralism? Edited by C.A.J. Coady". *Metaphilosophy* 39 (2):251–256.

Jenkins, K. (2017). "Rape Myths and Domestic Abuse Myths as Hermeneutical Injustices". *Journal of Applied Philosophy* 34 (2):191–205.

Jollimore, T. (2006). "Morally Admirable Immorality". *American Philosophical Quarterly* 43 (2):159–170.

Kant, I. (1996). *The Metaphysics of Morals.* Translated by M. Gregor. Cambridge University Press.

Kaufman, G. (2020). "Why Has R. Kelly Been in Jail for the Past Year?" *Billboard.* https://www.billboard.com/articles/business/legal-and-management/9430230/r-kelly-why-in-jail-for-year [Accessed: 19/04/2021]

Kauppinen, A. (2019). "Ideals and Idols: On the Nature and Appropriateness of Agential Admiration". In A. Archer and A. Grahlé (eds), *The Moral Psychology of Admiration* (pp. 29–44). Rowman and Littlefield.

Khoury, A., and Matheson, B. (2018). "Is Blameworthiness Forever?" *Journal of the American Philosophical Association* 4 (2):204–224.

Krauthammer, C. (1999). "Person of the Century....". *The Washington Post.* https://www.washingtonpost.com/wp-srv/WPcap/1999-12/31/066r-123199-idx.html [Accessed: 19/04/2021]

Kristjánsson, K. (2006). "Emulation and the Use of Role Models in Moral Education". *Journal of Moral Education* 35 (1):37–49.

Kutz, C. (2000). *Complicity: Ethics and Law for a Collective Age.* Cambridge University Press.

Lai, T-H. (2020). "Political Vandalism as Counter-Speech: A Defense of Defacing and Destroying Tainted Monuments". *European Journal of Philosophy* 28:602–616.

Landis, S.K., Sherman, M.F., Piedmont, R.L., Kirkhart, M.W., Rapp, E.M., and Bike, D.H. (2009). "The Relation between Elevation and Self-Reported Prosocial Behavior: Incremental Validity over the Five-Factor Model of Personality". *The Journal of Positive Psychology* 4 (1):71–84.

Leaming, B. (1982). *Polanski: His Life and Films.* Hamish Hamilton.

Lee, M.O. (1999). *Wagner: The Terrible Man and His Truthful Art.* University of Toronto Press.

Lee, S. (2017). "The Picasso Problem: Why We Shouldn't Separate the Art From the Artist's Misogyny". *Artspace.* https://www.artspace.com/magazine/interviews_features/art-politics/the_picasso_problem_why_we_shouldnt_separate_the_art_from_the_artists_misogyny-55120 [Accessed: 19/04/2021]

Lee, J.S., and Kwak, D.H. (2016). "Consumers' Responses to Public Figures' Transgression: Moral Reasoning Strategies and Implications for Endorsed Brands". *Journal of Business Ethics* 137 (1):101–113.

Leiter, B. (2018). "Blaming the Victim Is Apparently OK When the Accused in a Title IX Proceeding Is a Feminist Literary Theorist". *Leiter Reports.*

https://leiterreports.typepad.com/blog/2018/06/blaming-the-victim-is-apparently-ok-when-the-accused-is-a-feminist-literary-theorist.html [Accessed: 30/10/2018].

Levi, P. (1988). *The Drowned and the Saved*. Translated by R. Rosenthal. Simon & Schuster.

Lewis, H.B. (1971). *Shame and Guilt in Neurosis*. International Universities.

Liao, Shen-yi (2017). "Non-Aesthetic Reasons for Engaging with a Work". *Daily Nous*. (21/11/2017). https://dailynous.com/2017/11/21/philosophers-art-morally-troubling-artists/#Liao [Accessed: 19/04/2021]

Liao, S.M. (2006). "The Idea of a Duty to Love". *The Journal of Value Inquiry* 40 (1):1–22.

Liebow, N., and Glazer, T. (forthcoming). "White Tears: Emotion Regulation and White Fragility". *Inquiry*, 1–21.

Lim, C.-M. (2020). "Vandalizing Tainted Commemorations". *Philosophy and Public Affairs* 48 (2):185–216.

Lonsway, K.A., and Fitzgerald, L.F. (1994). "Rape Myths: In Review". *Psychology of Women Quarterly* 18:133–164.

Lopez, G. (2017). "The Battle over Confederate Statues, Explained". *Vox*. https://www.vox.com/identities/2017/8/16/16151252/confederate-statues-white-supremacists [Accessed: 19/04/2021]

Lyons, W.E. (1980). *Emotion*. Cambridge University Press.

MacDonald, H. (2019). "The Defenestration of Domingo". *Quillette*. (18/10/2020). https://quillette.com/2019/10/18/the-defenestration-of-domingo/ [Accessed: 1/4/2020].

Macnamara, C. (2015). "Reactive Attitudes as Communicative Entities". *Philosophy and Phenomenological Research* 90 (3):546–569.

Macnamara, C. (2020). "Guilt, Desert, Fittingness, and the Good". *Journal of Ethics* 24 (4):449–468.

Manne, K. (2017). *Down Girl: The Logic of Misogyny*. Oxford University Press.

Mason, M. (2003). "Contempt as a Moral Attitude". *Ethics* 113 (2):234–272.

Matheson, B. (2014). "Compatibilism and Personal Identity". *Philosophical Studies* 170 (2):317–334.

Matheson, B. (2017a). "More than a Feeling: The Communicative Function of Regret". *International Journal of Philosophical Studies* 25 (5):664–681.

Matheson, B. (2017b). "Alternative Possibilities, Volitional Necessities, and Character Setting". *Disputatio* 9 (45):287–307.

Matheson, B. (2019b). "Towards a Structural Ownership Condition on Moral Responsibility". *Canadian Journal of Philosophy* 49 (4):458–480.

Matheson, B. (2019a). "Should Aung San Suu Kyi's Nobel Peace Prize Be Revoked?' *Bij Nader Inzien* (18/3/2019). https://bijnaderinzien.org/2019/03/18/should-aung-san-suu-kyis-nobel-peace-prize-be-revoked/ [Accessed: 19/04/2021]

McColl, P. (2020). "Why Did We Remove Jimmy Savile Memorials While We Leave Slave Traders on Plinths?" https://petermccoll.wordpress.com/

McKenna, M. (2012). *Conversation and Responsibility*. Oxford University Press.

McPherson, T. (2015). "Why I Am a Vegan (and You Should Be One Too)". In *Philosophy Comes to Dinner* (pp. 73–91). Routledge.

Medina, J. (2011). "The Relevance of Credibility Excess in a Proportional View of Epistemic Injustice: Differential Epistemic Authority and the Social Imaginary". *Social Epistemology* 25 (1):15–35.

Miller, C.B. (2014). *Character and Moral Psychology*. Oxford University Press.

Miller, D. (1979). *Social Justice*. Oxford University Press.

Miller, D. (2001). *Principles of Social Justice*. Harvard University Press.

Mills, C.W. (2017). *Black Rights/White Wrongs: The Critique of Racial Liberalism*. Oxford University Press.

Mukerjee, M. (2010). *Churchill's Secret War: The British Empire and the Ravaging of India*. Basic Books.

Murdoch, I. (1970). *The Sovereignty of Good*. Routledge.

Nannicelli, T. (2020). *Artistic Creation and Ethical Criticism*. Oxford University Press.

National Trust for Historic Preservation (2018). "Statement on Confederate Memorials: Confronting Difficult History". https://savingplaces.org/press-center/media-resources/national-trust-statement-on-confederate-memorials-2017#.X_Qo09i2k2w [Accessed: 5/1/2021].

Nussbaum, M.C. (2001). *Upheavals of Thought: The Intelligence of Emotions*. Cambridge University Press.

Nussbaum, M.C. (2004). *Hiding from Humanity: Disgust, Shame, and the Law*. Princeton University Press.

Olsaretti, S. (ed.) (2003). *Desert and Justice*. Oxford University Press.

Oltermann, P. (2014). "Heidegger's 'Black Notebooks' Reveal Antisemitism at Core of His Philosophy". *The Guardian*. https://www.theguardian.com/books/2014/mar/13/martin-heidegger-black-notebooks-reveal-nazi-ideology-antisemitism [Accessed: 08/06/2018].

Otto, J. (2011). "Christoph Waltz Talks Working with Roman Polanski & Playing the 'Smuggest Character Ever' in 'Carnage'". *Indiewire*. https://www.indiewire.com/2011/12/christoph-waltz-talks-working-with-roman-polanski-playing-the-smuggest-character-ever-in-carnage-114055/ [Accessed: 19/04/2021]

Pacovská, K. (2018). "Love and the Pitfall of Moralism". *Philosophy* 93 (2):231–249.

Paharia, N., and Deshpandé, R. (2009). "Sweatshop Labor Is Wrong Unless the Jeans Are Cute: Motivated Moral Disengagement". Working Paper No. 09-079, Harvard Business School, Boston, MA 02163.

Paris, P. (2018). "The 'Moralism' in Immoralism: A Critique of Immoralism in Aesthetics". *British Journal of Aesthetics* 59 (1):13–33.

Pettigrove, G. (2004). "Unapologetic Forgiveness". *American Philosophical Quarterly* 41 (3):187–204.

Pettigrove, G., and Parsons, N. (2012). "Shame: A Case Study of Collective Emotion". *Social Theory and Practice* 38 (3):504–530.

Phillips, K. (2018). "Albert Einstein Decried Racism in America: His Diaries Reveal a Xenophobic Misogynistic Side". *The Washington Post.* https://www.washingtonpost.com/news/retropolis/wp/2018/06/13/albert-einstein-decried-racism-in-america-his-diaries-reveal-a-xenophobic-misogynistic-side/ [Accessed: 19/04/2021]

Poirier, A. (2010). "The Prurient Hounding of Roman Polanski Is over at Last". *The Guardian.* https://www.theguardian.com/commentisfree/cifamerica/2010/jul/12/roman-polanski-extradite-swiss-us [Accessed: 1/4/2020].

Pulver, A. (2010). "Chinatown: The Best Film of All Time". *The Guardian.* https://www.theguardian.com/film/2010/oct/22/best-film-ever-chinatown-season [Accessed: 11/11/2017].

Radzik, L. (2009). *Making Amends: Atonement in Morality, Law, and Politics.* Oxford University Press.

Rein, Irvin J., Kotler, P., and Stoller, M.R. (1997). *High Visibility: The Making and Marketing of Professionals into Celebrities.* NTC Publishing Group.

Riggs, G. (1998). "What Should We Do about Eduard Pernkopf's Atlas?" *Academic Medicine* 73 (4):380–386.

Rosen, C. (2020). "Portrait of a Lady on Fire Star Adèle Haenel Slams Roman Polanski's César Nominations". *Vanity Fair.* https://www.vanityfair.com/hollywood/2020/02/adele-haenel-roman-polanski

Rossi, B.C. (2020). "False Exemplars: Admiration and the Ethics of Public Monuments". *Journal of Ethics and Social Philosophy* 18 (1).

Scarantino, A., and de Sousa, R. (2018). "Emotion". In E.N. Zalta (ed.), *The Stanford Encyclopedia of Philosophy.* https://plato.stanford.edu/archives/win2018/entries/emotion/

Schindler, I., Paech, J., and Löwenbrück, F. (2015). "Linking Admiration and Adoration to Self-Expansion: Different Ways to Enhance One's Potential". *Cognition and Emotion* 29 (2):292–310.

Schindler, I., Zink, V., Windrich, J., and Menninghaus, W. (2013). "Admiration and Adoration: Their Different Ways of Showing and Shaping Who We Are". *Cognition and Emotion* 27:85–118.

Schmidtz, D. (2002). "How to Deserve". *Political Theory* 30 (6):774–799.

Schnall, S., Roper, J., and Fessler, D.M. (2010). "Elevation Leads to Altruistic Behavior". *Psychological Science* 21 (3):315–332.

Schroeder,M. (2010). "Value and theRightKind of Reason," in R. Shafer-Landau (ed.) *Oxford Studies in Metaethics 5* (pp. 25–55). Oxford: Oxford University Press.

Schulz, J. (2019). "Must Rhodes Fall? The Significance of Commemoration in the Struggle for Relations of Respect". *Journal of Political Philosophy* 27 (2):166–186.

Sen, M. (2015). "Gandhi Was a Racist Who Forced Young Girls to Sleep in Bed with Him". *Vice.* https://www.vice.com/en/article/ezj3km/gandhi-was-a-racist-who-forced-young-girls-to-sleep-in-bed-with-him [Accessed: 19/04/2021]

Sheffer, E. (2018). *Asperger's Children: The Origins of Autism in Nazi Vienna.* W. W. Norton.

Shotwell, A. (2016). *Against Purity: Living Ethically in Compromised Times.* University of Minnesota Press.

Sinnott-Armstrong, W. (1984). "'Ought' Conversationally Implies 'Can'". *Philosophical Review* 93 (2):249–261.

Skorupski, J. (2010). *The Domain of Reasons.* Oxford University Press.

Slapper, H. (2011). "Whatever His Crimes, Roman Polanski Deserves His Awards". *The Guardian.* (27/9/2011). https://www.theguardian.com/commentisfree/2011/sep/27/roman-polanski-lifetime-achievement-award [Accessed: 19/04/2021]

Slote, M.A. (1983). *Goods and Virtues.* Clarendon University Press.

Smith, A. (1759/2007). *The Theory of Moral Sentiments.* Cosimo.

Smith, L. (2021). *Emotional Heritage: Visitor Engagement at Museums and Heritage Sites.* Routledge.

Smuts, A. (2013). "The Salacious and the Satirical: In Defense of Symmetric Comic Moralism". *Journal of Aesthetic Education* 47 (4):45–62.

Sparrow, M., and Silberman, S. (2018). "On Hans Asperger, the Nazis, and Autism: A Conversation across Neurologies". *Thinking Person's Guide to Autism.* http://www.thinkingautismguide.com/2018/04/on-hans-asperger-nazis-and-autism.html [Accessed: 08/06/2018].

Spurgin, E. (2012). "Hey, How Did I Become a Role Model? Privacy and the Extent of Role-Model Obligations". *Journal of Applied Philosophy* 29 (2):118–132.

Stockdale, K. (2013). "Collective Resentment". *Social Theory and Practice* 39 (3):501–521.

Street, J. (2004). "Celebrity Politicians: Popular Culture and Political Representation". *The British Journal of Politics & International Relations* 6 (4):435–452.

Tappolet, C. (2016). *Emotions, Values, and Agency.* Oxford University Press.

Taylor, C. (2012). *Moralism: A Study of a Vice.* Acumen.

Taylor, R. (1970). *Good and Evil.* Macmillan.

The Nobel Peace Prize (1991). "Aung San Suu Kyi". https://www.nobelprize.org/nobel_prizes/peace/laureates/1991/ [Accessed: 15/05/2018].

Thomson, M. (2006). "Human Brands: Investigating Antecedents to Consumers' Strong Attachments to Celebrities". *Journal of Marketing* 70 (3):104–119.

Thrash, T.M., and Elliot, A.J. (2004). "Inspiration: Core Characteristics, Component Processes, Antecedents, and Function". *Journal of Personality and Social Psychology* 87 (6):957–973.

van de Ven, N. (2017). "Envy and Admiration: Emotion and Motivation Following Upward Social Comparison". *Emotion and Cognition* 31 (1):193–200.

van de Ven, N., Archer, A.T., and Engelen, B. (2019). "More Important and Surprising Actions of a Moral Exemplar Trigger Stronger Admiration and Inspiration". *The Journal of Social Psychology* 159 (4):383–397.

van de Ven, N., Zeelenberg, M., and Pieters, R. (2011). "Why Envy Outperforms Admiration". *Personality and Social Psychology Bulletin* 37 (6):784–795.

van Krieken, R. (2012). *Celebrity Society*. Routledge.

Velleman, J.D. (2009). *How We Get Along*. Cambridge University Press.

von Scheve, C., and Ismer, S. (2013). "Towards a Theory of Collective Emotions". *Emotion Review* 5 (4):406–413.

Vranas, Peter B.M. (2018). "'Ought' Implies 'Can' but Does Not Imply 'Must': An Asymmetry between Becoming Infeasible and Becoming Overridden". *Philosophical Review* 127 (4):487–514.

Wallace, M. (1990). *Invisibility Blues: From Pop to Theory*. Verso.

Walsh, P.W., and Lehmann, D. (2019). "Academic Celebrity". *International Journal of Politics, Culture, and Society* 34: 21–46.

Williams, B. (1981). *Moral Luck*. Cambridge University Press.

Williams, B. (1993). *Shame and Necessity*. University of California Press.

Wills, B., and Holt, J. (2017). "Art by Jerks". *Contemporary Aesthetics* 15 (1).

Wills, V. (2019). "Toward a Concept of Revolutionary Admiration: Marx and the Commune". In A. Archer and A. Grahlé (eds), *The Moral Psychology of Admiration* (pp. 113–128). Rowman and Littlefield.

Wolf, S. (1982). "Moral Saints". *Journal of Philosophy* 79 (8):419–439.

Wolf, S. (2010). "Good-for-nothings". *Proceedings and Addresses of the American Philosophical Association* 85 (2):47–64.

Wu, T. (2010). *The Master Switch: The Rise and Fall of Information Empires*. Atlantic Books.

Yaffe, G. (1999). "'Ought' Implies 'Can' and the Principle of Alternate Possibilities". *Analysis* 59 (3):218–222.

Yap, A. (2017). "Credibility Excess and the Social Imaginary in Cases of Sexual Assault". *Feminist Philosophy Quarterly* 3 (4)

Yee, A., Coombs, D.M., Hildebrandt, S., Seidelman, W.E., Coert, J.H., and Mackinnon, S.E. (2019). "Nerve Surgeons' Assessment of the Role of Eduard Pernkopf's Atlas of Topographic and Applied Human Anatomy in Surgical Practice". *Neurosurgery* 84 (2):491–498.

Zagzebski, L.T. (2015). "Admiration and the Admirable". *Proceedings of the Aristotelian Society* 89:205–221.

Zagzebski, L.T. (2017). *Exemplarist Moral Theory*. Oxford University Press.

Zaretsky, R. (2017). "Should Harvey Weinstein Make Us Rethink Roman Polanski. The French Say 'Non!'" *Forwards*. https://forward.com/culture/387082/should-harvey-weinstein-make-us-rethink-roman-polanski-the-french-say-non/ [Accessed: 16/11/2017].

Zimmerman, M.J. (1999). "The Moral Aspect of Nonmoral Goods and Evils". *Utilitas* 11 (1):1–15.

Index

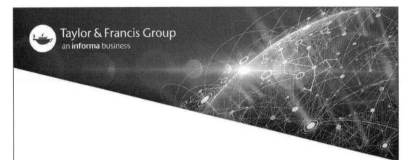